H21 565 495 X

8/12

BRACEGIRDLE, J.
EXHIBITION CANARIES

636.6'86

Hertfordshire
COUNTY COUNCIL
Community Information

6 JAN 2000

Please renew/return this item by the last date shown.

So that your telephone call is charged at local rate,
please call the numbers as set out below:

	From Area codes 01923 or 0208:	From the rest of Herts:
Renewals:	01923 471373	01438 737373
Enquiries:	01923 471333	01438 737333
Minicom:	01923 471599	01438 737599

L32b

EXHIBITION CANARIES

EXHIBITION CANARIES

by

Joe Bracegirdle

"Teach me to win when I can, but above all make me a good loser"

Distributor:
NIMROD BOOK SERVICES
P.O. Box 1, Liss, Hants.,
GU33 7PR, England.

© Joe Bracegirdle and Learnex (Publishers) Ltd., 1986

ISBN 086230 054 1

Typeset by Arrowhead Publishing

Produced and Published by Triplegate Ltd.,
Liss, Hants.,
England.

CONTENTS

Chapter		Page
	Monochrome Illustrations	vi
	Author's Preface	ix
1	The Wild Canary	1
2	Today's Exhibition Canaries	5
3	Breeding	39
4	Breeding Stock, Genetics and Colour	64
5	The Egg and its Development	78
6	Management — from Nest to Show Bench	96
7	Preparing for Exhibition	105
8	Green, Cinnamon and White Canaries	123
9	Type Canaries	128
10	Winter-Time Management	135
11	Food Values	142
12	Making your own Softfood	153
13	Canaries in Australia	162
14	Canary Ailments	168
15	Guide-lines for Judges	180
	Canary Terminology	185
	Index	188

MONOCHROME ILLUSTRATIONS

Figure		*Page*
1.1	The original Hartz Roller	2
2.1	Present-day Border Ideal	7
2.2	The original 'Cumberland Fancy', now called Borders	8
2.3	Unflighted variegated Yellow Border hen	10
2.4	Gloster Corona; note the amount of feathers in the crest	10
2.5	Gloster Corona Consort Ideal	12
2.6	An early Norwich Canary, similar to an Australian Plainhead	14
2.7	The ideal present-day Norwich	15
2.8	An early type of Yorkshire	18
2.9	An ideal present-day Yorkshire	19
2.10	Lizard Canary fault: 'overcapped'. This could be caused by pairing two capped birds together	21
2.11	Colour Canary	24
2.12	Start training young birds at an early stage	26
2.13	A Crested Canary	30
2.14	A Crest-bred; note quantity of feather on its brow	30
2.15	Drawing of the ideal Scotch Fancy produced in 1981 by the Old Varieties Canary Association	32
2.16	The present-day Belgian Fancy model	35
2.17	Fife Fancy Canary (Yellow Hen)	35
2.18	Lancashire Coppy of 1880	37
2.19	The London Fancy	38
3.1	Breeding card; essential for maintaining accurate records	41
3.2	Nest pans; wooden variety, earthenware type with a gripping rim	46
3.3	Faults in a Border Fancy; (a) position on perch (b) long flighted	50
3.4	Gloster Corona fault; split in crest	51
3.5	Norwich fault; narrow, mean, and flat above the beak	52
3.6	Sow thistle; very good to give feeding hens	56
3.7	Chickweed	58
3.8	Seeding dock	58
3.9	Ringing	63
3.10	Wooden Nest Pan (used in UK only)	63
4.1	Two types of bird bath and a hand held spray	67
4.2	Line breeding chart	72
5.1	After 18 hours of incubation, showing the head fold	80
5.2	After 36 hours of incubation showing eye divisions, mid brain, heart, and neural fold	80
5.3	After 72 hours of incubation	82
5.4	After 80 hours of incubation	85
5.5	After 96 hours of incubation	85

5.6	Five day old embryo	87
5.7	Embryo on the ninth day	89
5.8	On the tenth day of incubation	91
5.9	Shell cutting tooth of unborn chick	93
5.10	Drawing of a young chick two days before hatching	93
5.11	Drawing of a young bird showing feather growth	94
6.1	Adult variegated Yellow Border Hen	98
6.2	The start of today's Yorkshires	101
6.3	One method of making egg food	104
7.1	A Broken cap and a Clear cap Lizard of 1880 before colour feeding was introduced	106
7.2	A Border show cage	107
7.3	A Gloster show cage	108
7.4	A Norwich show cage	108
7.5	A Yorkshire show cage	109
7.6	Lizard and New Colour Canary show cage	111
7.7	A Roller song contest cage	116
7.8	Equipment for hand-washing canaries	117
7.9	Aviary Seed Hopper	121
7.10	Washing equipment	122
8.1	A yellow and Buff Green Yorkshire, and a Yellow Green Norwich of 1890	125
9.1	Table show at a club meeting night at the Barcelona Canary Club	130
9.2	Barcelona Canary Club show	131
9.3	The Australian Plainhead Canary; 1982 Standard of Excellence	133
9.4	Young Canaries (3 days old)	134
10.1	The correct way to hold a canary to examine its body	136
10.2	Brick-built birdroom	139
10.3	Useful birdroom aids	140
11.1	A mixture of canary seed and rape seed, which is darker	145
11.2	Plantain	149
11.3	Persicaria	151
11.4	Shepherd's Purse	151
11.5	Seeding Dock; excellent food for moulting canaries	152
12.1	Various feeders	157
12.2	Teazle heads and Plantain	157
12.3	Nest Box	160
12.4	Nest of chicks at nine days old	161
13.1	A 1900 Border	164
13.2	Typical Australian Canary Flight	166
14.1	Some useful medicines	169
14.2	Hospital cage	172
14.3	Giving a thorough spring cleaning	179
15.1	Crest Canary; very good crest and closely drawn on the legs	181
15.2	A show in progress	183

LIST OF COLOURED PLATES

Plate 1   Canaries 80 years ago

Plate 2   Lizard and London Fancy Canaries

Plate 3   Lancashire Coppy Canaries

Plate 4   Border Canaries

Plate 5   Yorkshire Canary — Variegated Buff Cock

Plate 6   Yorkshire Canary — Unflighted Variegated Buff Hen

Plate 7   The Ideal Norwich Canary
(Courtesy: Scottish Norwich Plainhead Canary Club)

Plate 8   Gloster Canary Hen, good type — dark vein in crest
(Courtesy: G R Wolfendale)

Plate 9   Colour Canary Champion Rose-Clear L L Robinson
(Photo: George Fry)

Plate 10 Team of Roller Canaries from Germany
(Photo: George Fry)

Plate 11 Blue Gloster Consort Hen with 3 Young White Consort Chicks
(Courtesy: G R Wolfendale)

AUTHOR'S PREFACE

I first started to breed canaries in 1935, and have continued to do so every year since then except for the period from September 1939 to November 1945 when I served in the Army during the war. I have been a Border panel judge since 1958. During the last thirty years I have written some two hundred articles and reports for the weekly journal *Cage and Aviary Birds.*

It has been my pleasure to have judged canaries at the National Shows of the U.K., Spain, Australia, and the U.S.A., and to have given lectures about type canaries while in these countries.

I have written this book *Exhibition Canaries* so that it can readily be understood and enjoyed, whether you have been keeping canaries for twenty years or twenty days, and trust that you will enjoy reading it as much as I did writing it.

During my forty-eight years of canary breeding there is just one thing that has always puzzled me, and that is, why so few ladies in the U.K. actively partake in this absorbing hobby. During my trip to the U.S.A. and visits in 1978, 1980 and 1982 to Australia, I was delighted to meet many very knowledgeable lady canary fanciers and judges.

I would like to thank Les Lockey for the photographs, H. Harrison and W. Chilton for their ready assistance, and my many fancier friends, both past and present, who have so willingly imparted their knowledge to me, which has helped me to write this book.

Joe Bracegirdle

Cheadle,
Cheshire.

The Wild Canary

CHAPTER 1

The Wild Canary

The recognised number one songbird in the avicultural world is, of course, the canary. This fact can be accurately traced back for 400 years or more, during which time many millions of people in most continents of the world have kept a canary as the family pet.

ORIGINS

The majority of the original wild canaries came into the U.K. 400 years ago. The canary — *Seria finch*– was found only on the islands of the eastern North Atlantic, the Canary and Cape Verde Islands, Madeira and the Azores. After a varied history the islands became a Spanish possession in 1479.

The original habitat was volcanic and wildly mountainous. The main island of the group, Teneriffe, was relatively small. The Serins built their nests of moss, feathers, or hair, among the dense vegetation of the steep slopes, and each pair produced several nests of young.

Three types of pigments are carried by the blood into the canary's feathers – yellow, black and brown, the original green colouring being a blend of yellow and black pigments.

The original canary, judging from old drawings, was a bird smaller in size than a sparrow, whose feathers were all a self buff green, with a browny-black shade of colour. They had short, black legs by comparison with the present-day canary, with a soft but quite musical song.

Increasing popularity

It was their song which first attracted the attention of the Spanish ships' captains on their visits to the Canary Isles, resulting in some of these singing birds being caught and taken back to Spain, where they were quickly admired by the nobility of that time. This admiration was such that in a few short years it became the accepted thing for all the houses of the wealthy merchants and noblemen to have a singing canary.

The canary is a bird which very readily acclimatises itself to a new environment, as is borne out by the fact that not only is it bred in both the

Figure 1.1 The original Hartz Roller

lowlands and the highlands of Scotland, but it is equally successful in the hottest parts of the Mediterranean countries, every state in the vast continent of Australia, and all over the Americas.

Canaries were, of course, first introduced into Europe for their song over 500 years ago, but the credit for breeding a canary solely as a really outstanding songbird must go to those early German pioneer breeders who were quick to realise the canary's song potential. They were also the very first breeders to acquire the genetic skill to develop the bird's song potential as we know it today. Credit for the early development of the canary must go to these Germans, especially the breeders who lived in the area of the Hartz mountains. It was from this area that the song of the canary was developed by those early breeders.

Progress

From those very humble early days we have the slow development of all the distinctive varieties and colours seen today in large numbers on the show bench. Such progress has been made in canary breeding in the last 100 years, with the various type canaries, the improvement in feather quality, and the almost countless development of new colour mutations, that it is extremely difficult to forecast what the next 50 years will bring.

I think that the most interesting development in canary breeding during the last decade throughout the world has been a general desire to breed canaries, be they type or song birds, to an international standard.

FROM 'SELFS' TO 'CLEARS'

Much has been done by fanciers to alter the canary since it was first introduced into Europe by the Spaniards in the fourteenth century. One feature which affects nearly all sections of the Fancy is the change in colour of the plumage. The original colour of the canary was a form of dull green not unlike that of our present-day Roller Canaries, except that the colour was inclined to be greyish in areas. But although it appears green to the human eye, the canary does not have the ability to produce green coloration; that which seems green is really a mixture of black and brown pigments superimposed on a yellow ground, and the balanced combination of these colours appears green to us.

Fouls

This balance is easily disturbed and can result in anything from a smoky-grey to a brownish-green colour; but whatever the result it still owes its origin to the three colours. Gradually a completely dark green colour, called a **Self** in the Fancy, gave place in birds having light coloured feathers.

These birds, known as **Fouls,** showed yellow colour in the light feathers. By careful selection the area of light feathers was increased, ranging from birds possessing more dark feathers to those with more light than dark feathers. These became known as **Variegated,** the former, "more dark than light" and the latter "more light than dark". Furthermore, we had birds with very slight dark marks, known as **Ticked,** and subsequently birds with no dark marks were known as **Clears.** These clear or light areas are the result of the suppression of the black and brown pigments. Because a bird is a Clear Yellow it does not mean that it does not possess the black and brown pigments. It is yellow because it is unable to express these pigments. This change from Dark Self to a Clear must have taken many generations of canaries before the established yellow colour of today was produced.

Clears

Now the Clear bird seems to predominate over all others. But this has meant a loss of beauty and interest in the canary. Few of today's Greens show the rich grass green of the birds bred years ago, and this is partly due to the craze for increased size. The majority of present-day canary breeds are larger than those of yesteryear. Very little of this increase is due to a larger frame or bone construction; it is due to 'larger feather'. Because of this the area of colour in each feather is greater which results in a change in the colour produced. Anyone wishing to breed birds of a rich grass green colour would first have to 'reduce' the size of the feather. Large feathering results in smoky pencil marks, because these areas become larger and the brown pigments are not completely covered by the black. By reducing the size of the feather the black and brown pencil marks become one, and the pencilling is sharp and more defined. One of the first mutations was an alteration of the black into brown, and because of its resemblance it has become known as the Cinnamon colour.

CHAPTER 2

Today's Exhibition Canaries

The development of the early song canary of 400 years ago, through selective breeding during the last 150 years, has resulted in the following **type** canaries being exhibited today; **Borders, Glosters, New Colours, Yorkshires, Norwich, Lizards, Crests, Frills, Scotch Fancies, Belgians, Fife Fancy** and, of course, the **Roller** which is bred purely for its beautiful soft mellow song. I have given these different varieties in their numerical order as they are found on the exhibition show bench today. The **Standards of Excellence** of these varieties are as detailed below.

THE BORDER CANARY

The Border Canary originated in the county of Cumberland, now called Cumbria, about 1850, and up to 1890 it was known as the Cumberland Fancy. In 1860 a meeting was held in Carlisle of all the breeders of this canary from the border counties; this resulted in its title of **The Border Canary** being created. At this meeting a specialist club for the variety was formed and took the name of **The Border Fancy Canary Club,** which is still very active.

The grand essentials of a Border Canary are **type** and **quality,** without which it is useless. The general appearance is that of a clean cut, lightly made, compact, well-proportioned, close feathered canary, showing no tendency to heaviness, roughness, or dullness, but giving the impression of fine quality and symmetry throughout.

Standard

Points		*Points 'A'*
10	**Head** — small, round and neat looking, beak fine, eyes central to roundness of head and body.	10

5

15	**Body** — Back well filled and nicely rounded, running in almost a straight line from the gentle rise over the shoulders to the point of the tail. Chest also nicely rounded, but neither heavy or prominent, the line gradually tapering to the vent.	15
10	**Wings** — Compact and carried close to the body, just meeting at the tips, at a point a little lower than the root of the tail.	10
5	**Legs** — of medium length, showing a little thigh, fine and in harmony with the other points, yet corresponding.	5
10	**Plumage** — Close, firm, fine in quality, presenting a smooth, glossy, silken appearance, free from frills or roughness.	5
5	**Tail** — Close packed and narrow, being nicely rounded and filled in at the root.	5
15	**Position** — Semi-erect, standing at an angle of 60 degrees.	15
15	**Colour** — Rich, soft and pure, as level in tint as possible throughout, but extreme depth and hardness, such as colour feeding gives, **is debarred.**	25
10	**Health** — Condition and cleanliness shall have due weight.	5
5	**Size** — But not to exceed 5½ inches in length.	5
___		___
100		100
___		___

N.B. Points 'A' are for Greens, Cinnamons, and Whites.

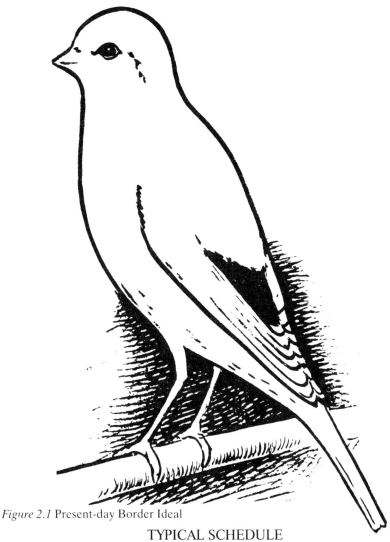

Figure 2.1 Present-day Border Ideal

TYPICAL SCHEDULE

The varieties found at shows may be seen from the schedule which follows, taken from the National Cage Bird Show:

CHAMPION BORDER CLASSES

74 Yellow Cock, clear or ticked
75 Yellow Hen, clear or ticked
76 Buff Cock, clear or ticked
77 Buff Hen, clear or ticked
78 Yellow Cock, variegated
79 Yellow Hen, variegated

Figure 2.2 The original 'Cumberland Fancy', now called Borders

80	Buff Cock, variegated
81	Buff Hen, variegated
82	Yellow Cock, 3-parts dark
83	Yellow Hen, 3-parts dark
84	Buff Cock, 3-parts dark
85	Buff Hen, 3-parts dark

Figure 2.3 Unflighted variegated Yellow Border hen

86	Yellow or Buff Cock, Cinnamon variegated
87	Yellow or Buff Hen, Cinnamon variegated
88	Cinnamon Yellow Cock, self or foul
89	Cinnamon Yellow Hen, self or foul
90	Cinnamon Buff Cock, self or foul
91	Cinnamon Buff Hen, self or foul
92	Green, Yellow Cock, self or foul
93	Green, Yellow Hen, self or foul
94	Green, Buff Cock, self or foul
95	Green, Buff Hen self or foul
96	Unflighted Yellow Cock, clear or ticked
97	Unflighted Yellow Hen, clear or ticked
98	Unflighted Buff Cock, clear or ticked
99	Unflighted Buff Hen, clear or ticked
100	Unflighted Yellow Cock, green, variegated
101	Unflighted Yellow Hen, green, variegated
102	Unflighted Buff Cock, green variegated
103	Unflighted Buff Hen, green, variegated
104	White Cock, clear or ticked
105	White Hen, clear or ticked
106	Blue, Fawn or variegated White Cock
107	Blue, Fawn or variegated White Hen
108	Even-marked Cock or Hen (including Whites).

Figure 2.4 Gloster Corona; note the amount of feathers in the crest

NOVICE BORDER CLASSES

109	Yellow Cock, clear or ticked
110	Yellow Hen, clear or ticked
111	Buff Cock, clear or ticked
112	Buff Hen, clear or ticked
113	Yellow Cock, variegated
114	Yellow Hen, variegated
115	Buff Cock, variegated
116	Buff Hen, variegated
117	Yellow or Buff Cock, 3-parts dark
118	Yellow or Buff Hen, 3-parts dark
119	Cinnamon, Yellow or Buff Cock, self or foul
120	Cinnamon, Yellow or Buff Hen, self or foul

121 **Green, Yellow or Buff Cock, self or foul**
122 **Green, Yellow or Buff Hen, self or foul**
123 **Unflighted Yellow Cock, clear or ticked**
124 **Unflighted Yellow Hen, clear or ticked**
125 **Unflighted Buff Cock, clear or ticked**
126 **Unflighted Buff Hen, clear or ticked**
127 **Unflighted Yellow Cock, variegated**
128 **Unflighted Yellow Hen, variegated**
129 **Unflighted Buff Cock, variegated**
130 **Unflighted Buff Hen, variegated**
131 **White Cock, any variety**
132 **White Hen, any variety**

THE GLOSTER CANARY

The Gloster Canary originated in the county of Gloucester during the late nineteen-twenties. Its big brothers were, of course, the Crest Canaries. There are two distinct varieties; *(a)* the **Corona,** which has the Crests, and **(b)** the **Consort,** which has a normal type head. These two distinct names for the Gloster were first suggested by the late A. W. Smith.

Standard

Corona	*Points*
Corona — Neatness, regular unbroken round shape, eye discernable,	15
with definite centre	5
Body — Back well filled and wings laying close thereto. Full neck. Chest nicely rounded without prominence.	20
Tail — Closely folded, well carried	5
Plumage — Close, firm, giving a clear appearance of good quality and natural colour.	15
Carriage — Alert, quick, lively movement.	10
Legs and Feet — Medium length, no blemish.	5
Size — Tendency to the diminutive.	15
Condition — Health and cleanliness.	10
	100

11

Figure 2.5 Gloster Corona Consort Ideal

Consort	*Points*
Consort — Head broad, round at every point with good rise over centre of skull.	15
Eyebrow — Heavy showing brow.	5
Body — Back well filled and wings laying close thereto. Full neck, chest nicely rounded without prominence.	20
Tail — Closely folded and well carried.	5
Plumage — Close, firm, giving a clear-cut appearance of good quality and good natural colour.	15
Carriage — Alert, quick, lively movement.	10
Legs and Feet — Medium length, no blemish.	5
Size — Tendency to the diminutive.	15
Condition — Health and cleanliness.	10
	100

Open Show
Schedule of Classes

GLOSTER CLASSES

Ch.	Nov.	
133	154	**Buff Corona Cock Flighted**
134	155	**Buff Corona Hen Flighted**
135	156	**Buff Consort Cock Flighted**
136	157	**Buff Consort Hen Flighted**
137	158	**Buff Corona Cock Unflighted**
138	159	**Buff Corona Hen Unflighted**
139	160	**Buff Consort Cock Unflighted**
140	161	**Buff Consort Hen Unflighted**
141	162	**Buff Three Parts Dark Corona Ck, or Hen Flighted**
142	163	**Buff Three Parts Dark Consort Ck, or Hen Flighted**
143	164	**Buff Three Parts Dark Corona Ck, or Hen Unflighted**
144	165	**Buff Three Parts Dark Consort Ck, or Hen Unflighted**
145	166	**Yellow Corona or Yellow Grizzle Cock Flighted or Unflighted**
146	167	**Yellow Corona or Yellow Grizzle Hen Flighted or Unflighted**
147	168	**Yellow Consort Cock Flighted or Unflighted**
148	169	**Yellow Consort Hen Flighted or Unflighted**
149	179	**Visual Cinnamon, Buff or Yellow Corona Cock or Hen Flighted or Unflighted**
150	171	**Visual Cinnamon, Buff or Yellow Consort Cock or Hen Flighted or Unflighted**
151	172	**White or Allied Corona Cock or Hen Flighted or Unflighted**
152	173	**White or Allied Consort Cock or Hen Flighted or Unflighted**
153	170	**Buff Clear or Grizzle Corona Cock or Hen Flighted or Unflighted**

THE NORWICH CANARY

The Norwich Canary was brought to England in 1750 by the Flemish refugees who were fleeing their native homeland due to persecution by the Spanish. They landed in Norfolk, and settled in and around Norwich, where there were already Flemish people living.

Over several decades the local people also commenced to breed this particlar type of canary and eventually called it the **Norwich Canary.** Even today, after some 200 years of breeding, East Anglia is still the centre for all genuine Norwich breeders. The Norwich of 1750 was a very much smaller bird, being only some five inches long, and today's bird is the result of selective breeding by very knowledgeable fanciers.

The first Specialist society for this variety started in 1901 and is called the **Norwich Plainhead Club** (N.P.C.), and other Specialist clubs came along later; the present Norwich started in 1900.

Figure 2.6 An early Norwich Canary, similar to an Australian Plainhead

Standard

Colour — Bright, rich, pure and level throughout.

Shape — **Head** — Round, full and neat.

Neck — Short and thick.

Body — Short and cobby, with wide back well filled in.

Chest — Deep, broad and full.

Feather — Soft and silky, with brilliancy and compactness.

Wings and Tail — Short, compact, with good carriage.

Size — Well proportioned.

Beak — Short and stout (clear).

Legs — Well set back.

Figure 2.7 The ideal present-day Norwich

Feet — Perfect.

Condition — Health, cleanliness and sound feather. Streaked beak and marked legs not to be a disqualification, but count against the bird to its extent.

Scale of Points for Judging

Type	.	.	.	.	**25**
Head	.	.	.	.	**10**
Neck	.	.	.	.	**10**
Wings	.	.	.	.	**10**
Tail	.	.	.	.	**5**

Legs and Feet	.	.	.	.	**5**
Condition	.	.	.	.	**10**
Quality of Feather	.	.	.	.	**10**
Colour	.	.	.	.	**10**
Staging	.	.	.	.	**5**

(Ideal length, 6 to 6¼ inches)

Total **100**

Open Show
Schedule of Classes

CHAMPION NORWICH CLASSES

1 Yellow Cock, clear or ticked
2 Yellow Hen, clear or ticked
3 Buff Cock, clear or ticked
4 Buff Hen, clear or ticked
5 Yellow Cock, marked, var. or self
6 Yellow Hen, marked, var. or self
7 Buff Cock, marked, var. or self
8 Buff Hen, marked, var. or self
9 Unflighted Yellow Cock, clear or ticked
10 Unflighted Yellow Hen, clear or ticked
11 Unflighted Buff Cock, clear or ticked
12 Unflighted Buff Hen, clear or ticked
13 Unflighted Yellow Cock, marked, var. or self
14 Unflighted Yellow Hen, marked, var. or self
15 Unflighted Buff Cock, marked, var. or self
16 Unflighted Buff Hen, marked, var. or self
17 Cinnamon Yellow Cock, self or foul
18 Cinnamon Yellow Hen, self or foul
19 Cinnamon Buff Cock, self or foul
20 Cinnamon Buff Hen, self or foul
21 White, Blue or Fawn, clear, var. or self, Cock or Hen

NOVICE NORWICH CLASSES

22 Yellow Cock, any variety
23 Yellow Hen, any variety
24 Buff Cock, any variety
25 Buff Hen, any variety
26 Unflighted Yellow Cock, any variety
27 Unflighted Yellow Hen, any variety
28 Unflighted Buff Cock, any variety
29 Unflighted Buff Hen, any variety
30 Cinnamon, Yellow or Buff, self or foul, Cock or Hen

16

THE YORKSHIRE CANARY

As its name implies, the Yorkshire Canary originated in the industrial heartlands of Yorkshire in about 1850. It is commonly accepted that most Yorkshire men have opinions of their own, so it was not surprising that these early Yorkshire fanciers were responsible for producing a type of canary which was distinctly different to any other variety known at that time.

Those early Yorkshire Canaries were all very tall and slim, and, it was said, could easily be passed through a wedding ring, and remained like that for many years. In about 1875 the first attempt was made to draw up a **standard of excellence** for this variety, since which at various times alterations have been made to the *standard,* until we have today's distinctive "Gentleman of the Fancy'.

The first Yorkshire Specialist Society to be formed was the Yorkshire Canary Club in 1894, in Bradford, which is still very active today and, since then, at various times, other specialist area societies have come into being.

Standard	*Points*
Head — Full, round and cleanly defined. Back skull deep and carried back in line with rise of shoulders. Eye as near centre of head as possbile. Shoulders proportionately broad, rounded and carried well up to, and gradually merging into, the head. Breast full and deep, corresponding to width and rise of shoulders carried up full to base of beak which should be neat and fine.	20
Body — Well rounded and gradually tapering to tail.	10
Position — Attitude erect with fearless carriage, legs long without being stilty and slight lift behind.	25
Feather — Close, short and tight. Wings proportionately long and evenly carried down the centre of the back, and firmly set on a compact and closely folded tail.	25
Size — Length approximately 6¾ inches with corresponding symmetrical proportions.	10
Condition — Health, cleanliness and sound feather; colour pure and level.	10
	100

17

Figure 2.8 An early type of Yorkshire

Open Show
Schedule of Classes

YORKSHIRE CLASSES

Ch.	Nov.	
31	53	Yellow Cock, clear, ticked or lightly var.
32	54	Yellow Hen, clear, ticked or lightly var.
33	55	Buff Cock, clear, ticked, or lightly var.
34	56	Buff Hen, clear, ticked or lightly var.
35	57	Yellow Cock, Green, even, uneven or variegated, self or foul
36	58	Yellow Hen, Green, even, uneven or variegated, self or foul
38	60	Buff Hen, Green, even, uneven or variegated, self or foul
39	61	Yellow or Buff Ck. Cinn. ticked, marked or var., self or foul
40	62	Yellow or Buff Hen, Cinn. ticked, mkd. or var., self or foul

18

Figure 2.9 An ideal present-day Yorkshire

41	63	Unflighted Yellow Cock, clear, ticked or lightly var.
42	64	Unflighted Yellow Hen, clear, ticked or lightly var.
43	65	Unflighted Buff Cock, clear, ticked or lightly var.
44	66	Unflighted Buff Hen, clear, ticked or lightly var.
45	67	Unflighted Yellow Cock, Green, even, uneven or var. self or foul
46	68	Unflighted Yellow Hen, Green, even, uneven or var. self or foul
47	69	Unflighted Buff Cock, Green, even, uneven or var. self or foul
48	70	Unflighted Buff Hen, Green, even, uneven or var. self foul
49	71	Unflighted Yellow or Buff Cock, Cinnamon ticked, marked or var. self or foul
50	72	Unflighted Yellow or Buff Hen, Cinnamon ticked, marked or var. self foul
51	73	White, Blue or Fawn, Cock or Hen
52	—	Green, non-colour-fed, self or foul, Cock or Hen

19

THE ROLLER CANARY

There are records of the Roller Canary being bred in the U.K. going as far back as 1650. It had been brought over from Europe because of its truly wonderful song. Over the years since then the singing ability of the Roller has gradually been improved and extended, until we have today's 'Master of Song', and this, in many ways, has been the result of European breeders' skill in song development and perfection. Because the song of the Roller was first developed by the Germans in the Hartz Mountain area – hence the name of a Hartz Roller song Canary – earlier than 1650, naturally we have accepted some of their descriptions. In the present-day songs we have the high, deep and light passages, which are called **Tours.** In the higher tours the music is inferior to the medium, in the deeper tours it is best, so far as purity of tone is concerned.

We may, therefore, classify the melody into the three following divisions:

Higher Pitched Tours	**Fair**
Medium or Middle Tours	**Good**
Deep Tours	**Very Good**

Here are just a few of the Roller's lovely notes: **Bell, Hollow Bell, Schockel, Flutes, Gluck.** It is interesting to note that the Roller sings all its many melodious notes with its beak partly open, and its throat and feathers extended and vibrating. Most young Roller cocks soon learn how to sing **Flutes.** This is quite the opposite to the **Gluck,** which many birds have difficulty with; other notes which, when sung properly are very pleasant to hear, are the **Hollow roll** and **Water Roll.** It is interesting to note that it is generally the end of September or early October before young birds commence to sing the **Bass** note. When training young cocks to sing they are kept in a single cage and put in a cabinet holding twelve such cages; in the centre cage is placed an adult cock of outstanding singing ability, and he acts as song-master for the young cocks to imitate their reproduction of song, the hope being that as they will not hear badly sung notes they will only learn the correct ones. The first Roller Specialist Society, the **National Roller Canary Association,** was formed in 1909.

THE LIZARD CANARY

This canary originated in France and exactly just how its feather pattern mutation occurred is not very clear; it is the only canary which has such distinctive plumage. It is quite true to say that its feather pattern of **Spangles** and **Rowings** has not changed at all in over 250 years that it has been bred in the U.K. Colour feeding is a more recent practice. The Lizard Canary was brought to England about 1750 by the Huguenots who came from France because of religious persecution.

Figure 2.10 Lizard Canary fault: 'overcapped'. This could be caused by pairing two capped birds together

In 1945, at the end of the war, there were only some eight or nine pairs of true Lizards left in the world, and they were all in the U.K. A few admirers of this canary met together and formed the **Lizard Canary Association** with a view to saving it from extinction. So successful has it been that today Lizards are bred all over Europe, U.S.A. and Australia. There are specialist clubs now in both Australia and America. They call their **Yellows 'Golds'** and the **Buffs 'Silvers',** due to them being a colour fed canary.

There are three categories of Lizard; *(a)* **Clear Cap,** which, as it implies, must have **no** dark feathers in it; *(2) Broken Cap,* which *does* have dark feathers in its cap; *(c)* **Non Cap,** which must **not** have **any** light coloured feathers on its head.

When breeding you should, *(a)* pair Gold to Silver, and *(b)* Clear Cap or a Broken Cap to a Non Cap. **Never** pair two capped birds together, because the caps of their young will come too far down the back of their necks and will thus be overcapped. One of the main attractions of a Lizard is the fact that it is a dark ground bird, with a black beak, legs and feet, but which has a lovely light-coloured head which, having been colour fed, is a complete contrast to the rest of the bird.

As a nest feathered bird the young Lizard is heavily striped on its back and flanks, and other than the cap, it appears quite similar to other young canaries. After its nest feather moult, it is seen in its ideal state of plumage as regards show condition. In its second and subsequent years, its feathers tend to show a certain amount of whitish tinge in its tail, flight feathers and its spangling feathers which, from an exhibition standard, counts against it. The amount of feather colour deterioration really does, to a large extent, depend on the skill and the knowledge of the particular fancier.

21

The late Ernest Nicholson of Stockport, Cheshire, many times exhibited Lizards that were three or four years old, still had perfect feathers, and were very worthy class winners. In 1968, with an overyear **Gold Clear Capped** cock, he won a **Gold Medal** for **Best Lizard** at the C.O.M. Show held in Hamburg, West Germany.

Standard	*Points*
Spangles — for regularity and distinctness	25
Feather Quality — for tightness and silkiness	15
Ground Colour — for depth and evenness	10
Breast — for extent and regularity of rowings	10
Wings and Tail — for neatness and darkness	10
Cap — for neatness and shape	10
Covert Feathers — for lacings	5
Eyelash — for regularity and clarity	5
Beak, Legs and Feet — for darkness	5
Steadiness and Staging —	5
	100

Open Show
Schedule of Classes

Ch.	Nov.	
221	232	Gold Cock, clear or nearly clear cap
222	233	Silver Cock, Clear or nearly clear cap
223	234	Gold Cock, Broken cap
224	235	Silver Cock, Broken cap
225	236	Gold Hen Clear or nearly clear cap
226	237	Silver Hen Clear or nearly clear cap
227	238	Gold Hen Broken cap
228	239	Silver Hen Broken cap
229	240	Gold or Silver Cock or Hen, non or nearly non cap, any age

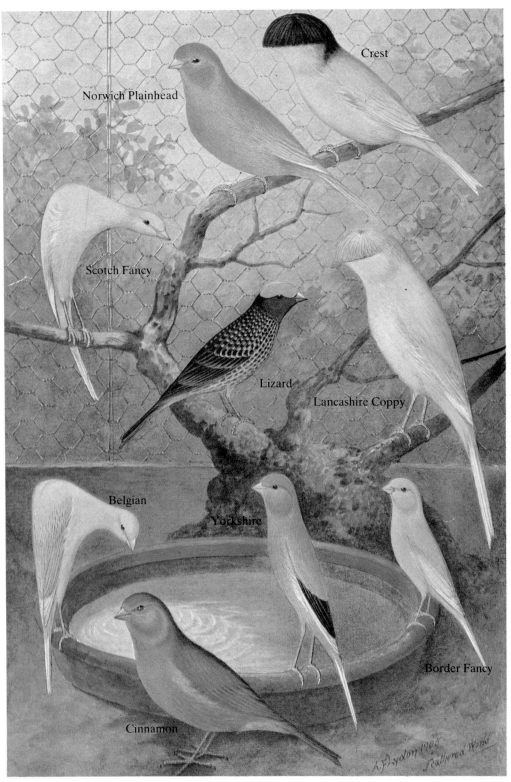

Plate 1   Canaries 80 years ago

Clear Capped
Gold Lizard

Broken Capped
Silver Lizard

Jonque London Fancy

F. Lydon.

Plate 2   Lizard and London Fancy Canaries

Yellow Coppy

Buff Plainhead

A.F.Lydon.

Plate 3   Lancashire Coppy Canaries

Variegated
yellow green
hen

Three parts
dark green

Self green
yellow hen

Clear white
buff hen

Plate 4   Border Canaries

Plate 5   Yorkshire Canary — Variegated Buff Cock

Plate 6   Yorkshire Canary — Unflighted Variegated Buff Hen

Plate 7   The Ideal Norwich Canary   (Courtesy: Scottish Norwich Plainhead Canary Club)

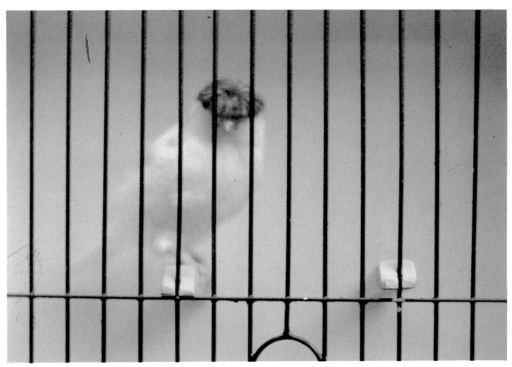

Plate 8   Gloster Canary Hen, good type — dark vein in crest
(Courtesy: G R Wolfendale)

Plate 9   Colour Canary Champion Rose-Clear L L Robinson
(Photo: George Fry)

Plate 10   Team of Roller Canaries from Germany
(Photo: George Fry)

Plate 11   Blue Gloster Consort Hen with 3 Young White Consort Chicks
(Courtesy: G R Wolfendale)

230   241   **Gold Cock or Hen, overyear**
231   242   **Silver Cock or Hen, overyear**

NEW COLOUR CANARIES

Red Factor Canaries, as they were first called, all originate from a Hybrid cock which had been bred from a South American Hooded Siskin cock paired to a canary hen which, when used to breed from, was found to be fertile. These young cocks were called **F1 hybrids.** It is interesting to note that the first Hooded Siskin Cross Canary hybrid bred, which was found to be fertile, occurred in 1926, and it was found in 1930 that both sexes of the Orange Canary bred from hybrid were fertile. When the F1 was paired back to a canary hen, the resulting young were called F2 hybrids. By the time that F4 generations had been bred and moulted out, we now had a Red Canary, hence the name of Red Factor Canaries.

Whilst U.K. Red Factor breeders were busy improving the colour of their birds, so too were many other fellow breeders in many European countries, so it was no surprise that it was our European friends who were to the forefront in producing many of today's new colour mutations from those early Red Factor Canaries.

During the last 35 years of selective and scientific breeding the **New Colour Canary** has truly been acknowledged throughout the world. I will now give in everyday language a breakdown of **Lipochrome Colouring** and **Melanistic Colouring,** starting with judging standards.

Judging Standards

Clears:	*Points*
Lipochrome Colouring	50
Degree of Frosting	10
Type	30
Condition and Feather Quality	10
	100

Selfs:	
Lipochrome Colouring	25
Melanistic Colouring	25
Degree of Frosting	10
Type	30
Condition and Feather Quality	10
	100

Figure 2.11 Colour Canary

Specific Standards

1. For the time being the existing pictorial model will apply, but this will be reviewed at next year's Convention.
2. The ideal length of a coloured canary is 5″.
3. Lipochrome Colouring
   (a) Red. Colour to be a bright rich fiery red, evenly distributed throughout the plumage.
   (b) Rose. Colour to be a bright deep rich pink, evenly distributed throughout the plumage.
   (c) Gold. Colour to be of a bright yellow, showing maximum optical blue. *Faults:* Tendency of colour to be orangy yellow.
   (d) Dominant White. Good clean white. *Faults:* Red or Yellow lipochrome appearing in the plumage.
   (e) Recessive White. As the action of this mutation is to completely mask all other traces of lipochrome colouring, nothing can be done either to improve or, alternatively, to cause a deterioration.
   (f) Ivory White. Good, clean white. *Faults:* whilst the ivory factor will normally mask the yellow lipochrome, often seen in the flight feathers of dominant white birds, it does tend to accentuate any red or yellow lipochrome present in the body feathers.

24

(g) *Ivory Gold.* A pleasant lemon yellow colouring showing maximum optical blue. *Faults:* Tendency to an orange-yellow colour.

General faults covering all ground colours:

(a) Uneven depth and distribution of colour.

(b) Dullness in colour.

4. Melanistic Colouring

Where applicable, i.e. where melanin pigment should be present, melanins to be distinct over the head, back and flanks, progressing round into the chest area. Optical blue (reduction of brown) factor to be present.

Faults

(a) Pencilling too coarse or faint and/or missing from flanks.

(b) Light colouring on feet, legs and beak, where dark colouring is called for. Alternatively, dark coloured horny areas where light coloration is called for. (These are covered under general standards for the various mutations later in this text).

(c) The light area local to the vent must be kept to a minimum with the obvious exception of the dimorphics.

(d) No foul feathers or areas of variegation to be allowed in self birds. A bird with any such fault to be immediately disqualified.

5. Degree of Frosting

(a) *Non Frosted.* All birds ideally should show no frosting whatever, but when this is present, it must be kept to an absolute minimum. *Faults:* Too much frosting, particularly round the neck and on the back.

(b) *Frosted.* Clear distinct frosting should be present, and evenly divided over the whole plumage. *Faults:* Irregular distribution of frosting often seen as either a frost-free chest or heavily frosted neck and back.

(c) *Dimorphic.* All must show the requirements of dimorphism, i.e. only four colour points: face, shoulders, rump and chest. To be specific, I will itemise these areas further. *Hens:* Face to show 'eyebrows only'. Colour not to run from eye to eye nor down to cheeks. *Cocks:* The face to show a blaze typical of a goldfinch, i.e. an area of coloration extending centrally from the beak and should be as restricted as possible. *Shoulders:* Small distinct area on shoulders only. Colour not to extend to wing flights. *Rump:* Small distinct area on top of rump, not to extend to back or body. *Chest:* Slight area centrally on chest not to flow up or down to head or under body. Remainder of body plumage, wings and tail to show bright clean white in clear varieties with corresponding colouring in self varieties. The colour points of cocks will be enlarged in comparison to hens. *Faults:* (Hens particularly)

(i) Colouring above the beak, on forehead, between beak and on the breast, running into wing flights.

(ii) Rough feathering.

25

Figure 2.12 Start training young birds at an early age

6. Feather quality and condition
Plumage to be close and firm in texture, presenting a smooth, silky appearance giving a clear-cut contour to body. The bird to be in full bloom of perfect health, clean, jaunty, bouncing in a steady manner.
7. Type
  (a) *Body outline:* Short and full to conform with agreed outline. Back well filled in showing a slight rise transversely. Chest broad and full, giving a nicely rounded front at an angle of 45% approximately to the perch.
  (b) *Head:* A full forehead rising from a short neat beak, to be well rounded over and across the skull. Eyes distinct, clear and bright.
  (c) *Neck:* Short and distinct, flowing neatly from back skull on to shoulders and from a full throat into chest.
  (d) *Wings:* Short and well braced, meeting nicely at tips to rest lightly, yet closely, on rump. (Tips of wings to end on rump). Flights to rest together, neatly tapering off gradually along wings.
  (e) *Tail:* Complete, short and tightly packed, well filled in at root. To be carried rigidly, giving an all in line appearance to the body.
  (f) *Legs and Feet:* Legs set well back, free from scale; feet perfect, all nails showing.

26

Individual Standards

Clears
All birds, regardless of ground colour, must comply with the specific standard relating to lipochrome colour, degree of frosting, and so on. Variegation is permitted in all varieties with the exception of dimorphic, where birds showing more than one tick mark of melanistic pigment must be disqualified.

Variegation is defined as follows:

Clear: A bird showing no melanistic pigment in its plumage whatever.
Ticked: A bird with one dark mark in its plumage coverable by a one new pence piece.
Variegated: A bird having more than one tick mark of melanin pigment in excess of that which can be covered by a one pence piece, up to a foul bird with one clear feather.

N.B. Dark coloration of the horny areas must be discounted. In all classes where a bird is considered equal in all areas to a ticked or variegated bird, the clear bird will take preference.

Selfs: All varieties must conform with the specific standards regarding lipochrome colour, and degree of frosting, and so on, as well as the specific rules for all self varieties. Individual varieties should conform to the following rules:

Brown and Green: To show maximum deep coloured pencilling which should be distinct. Optical blue factor giving a reduction of phaeomelanin brown. Green birds to show jet black horny areas. Brown birds to have flesh coloured horny areas.

Isabel and Agate: The same standard as for brown and green except that the pencilling should be extremely fine. The horny areas in both instances to be flesh coloured.

Brown and Pastel: Distinct but fine pencilling with an overlaying brown suffusion. Flesh coloured horny areas.

Isabel Pastel: Pencilling absent, brown suffusion present but diluted.

Green Pastel: Pencilling to be broad but distinct and of dark grey colour except in the wings and tail, where a broad, pale silvery grey bar, flanked with a narrower bar of dark grey on either side, should be visible, i.e. showing maximum grey wing effect. Horny areas to be dark with a black tip to the beak and each claw.

Agate Pastel: Pencilling to be as fine as possible and of a dark grey colour. Horny areas flesh coloured.

Brown Satinette: Maximum brown pencilling. Flesh coloured horny areas.

Agate and Green Satinette: Extremely fine brown pencilling. Flesh coloured horny areas.

Brown and Isabel Opal: Extremely fine brown pencilling. Flesh coloured horny areas.

Green Opal: Pencilling to be distinct and broad, of a silvery grey colour. Horny areas to be jet black.

Agate Opal: As with the green opal, but pencilling to be finer and horny areas flesh coloured.

Brown and Green Ino: Pencilling to be broad and distinct, with phaeomelanin on feather tips expressed to the maximum. Horny areas flesh coloured.

Isabel and Agate Ino: Standard as for green and brown ino except that all melanins will be finer and less distinct.

Classification of birds

There are two feather types:

Hard	Yellow	Red	Gold
Soft	Buff	Apricot	Silver

Variegated birds
Variegation is determined by the **melanin** colour carried by the bird. Melanin is the black and brown coloured feathers.

Ticked
A ticked bird is classified as having only one patch of visible melanin,without handling the bird,which could be covered by a one pence piece. The rest of the bird is covered in feathers of its ground colour.

Lightly variegated
Less than 50% melanin or more than 50% ground colour.

Self birds
Covered 100% in melanin, nil ground colour visible.

Clear birds
Covered 100% ground colour, nil melanin visible. Note Buff Clears could show frosting, i.e. white tipped feathers such as the Apricot Red Buff, Red Ground Lipochrome.

Reds

Lipochrome
There are the clear series of Red Factor, i.e. Clear, Ticked or variegated Reds, Apricots and Mosaic.

TODAY'S EXHIBITION CANARIES

Melanins
These are the self dark series of Red Factors, i.e. Bronze, Cinnamon or
Mosaic Bronze or Cinnamon. Variegated dark birds can only be shown in the
Variegated Lipochrome classes.

Open Show
Schedule of Classes

CLEAR, TICKED OR VARIEGATED CLASSES

Ch.	Nov.	
175	198	**Flighted Red Orange Cock**
176	199	**Unflighted Clear Red Orange Cock**
177	200	**Unflighted Ticked or Variegated Red Orange Cock**
178	201	**Flighted Apricot Cock**
179	202	**Unflighted Clear Apricot Cock**
180	203	**Unflighted Ticked or Variegated Apricot Cock**
181	204	**Red Orange Hen**
182	205	**Apricot Hen**
183	206	**Non Frosted Rose Cock or Hen**
184	207	**Frosted Rose Cock or Hen**
185	208	**Clear or Ticked Dimorphic Cock or Hen**
186	209	**A.O.V. Clear or Ticked Variegated Cock or Hen**

ORANGE GROUND SELFS

187	210	**Frosted Bronze or Brown Cock or Hen**
188	211	**Non Frosted Bronze or Brown Cock or Hen**
189	212	**Isabel or Agate Cock or Hen**
190	213	**Ino or Satinette Cock or Hen**
191	214	**A.O.V. Orange Ground Cock or Hen**

ROSE GROUND SELFS

192	215	**Bronze, Brown, Isabel or Agate Cock or Hen**
193	216	**A.O.V. Rose Ground Cock or Hen**

GOLD OR SILVER GROUND SELFS

194	217	**Pastel or Opal Cock or Hen**
195	218	**Ino Cock or Hen**
196	219	**Satinette Cock or Hen**
197	220	**A.O.V. Gold or Silver Ground Cock or Hen**

NB. Self Dimorphics can be exhibited in either their relevant mutation Class or the
A.O.V. Class for each ground colour. Gold and Silver Ivories and Recessive
Whites should be exhibited in the relevant Gold or Silver classes.

29

Figure 2.13 A Crested Canary

Figure 2.14 A Crest-bred; note quantity of feather on its brow

CREST CANARIES

The first record of a Crest mutation was in 1770, and the present-day Crest goes back to 1890. Very few Crest Canaries are now exhibited in the U.K. but I am pleased to say that they are quite popular in Australia; I have seen them in every state out there that I have visited.

Characteristics

The main feature of this variety is, of course, its Crest but, as with this breed, there are plain headed varieties as well, which are called Crest-breds, which are the breeding partners for the actual Crested bird, and are essential for the correct breeding.

The Crested Canary is quite a large bird and thus has a lot of feathering on both the head and the body. It should have a very large head, with a short thick neck, and a broad deep body. It should have a low position on the perch with its legs well set back. The actual Crest should be as large as is possible, with broad, leafy feathers which should form an even all round appearance with a small neat centre, and form a perfect arc over the eyes and beak.

Open Show
Schedule of Classes

261 **Crest Cock or Hen**
262 **Crest-bred Cock or Hen**
263 **Unflighted Crest Cock or Hen**
264 **Unflighted Crest-bred Cock or Hen**
265 **Novice Crest Cock or Hen**
266 **Novice Crest-bred Cock or Hen**

SCOTCH FANCY

The Scotch Fancy originated about 1800, with an attempt being made in 1880 to form a *standard* for it; it actually originated from the Belgian Fancy. In the early days it was often called a bird of circle because of its shape and its very upright stance; it was also called the **Glasgow Don.**

Characteristics

It really is a canary of position which has its own fair, long, slim body forming what could be called a half circle. It should have a round, well curved back and have a clean-cut underbody. It should have a small, narrow shaped head, only seen in this type of bird, the actual neck to be long and thin, which reaches well forward when the bird is standing in an ideal position. The shoulders should be the highest point, with no hollowness, and sloping away to a long closely compact tail which bends away under the perch, which gives the appearance of the bird forming a circle.

The bird should have a free and active carriage on the perch, the legs to create life and movement as it works the perch. The decline in popularity among breeders is associated with its poor fertility record.

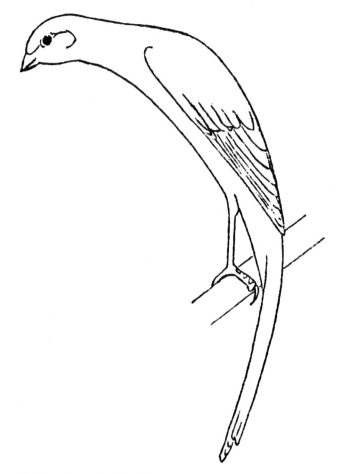

Figure 2.15 Drawing of the ideal Scotch Fancy produced
in 1981 by the Old Varieties Canary Association

Standard   Points

Shape — Body long, curved and tapering in a half circle,
concave below with a clean outline, the feathering
to be short and close.   20

Head and Neck — Small, neat and narrow head,
long tapering neck.   10

Shoulders and Back — High, narrow, rounded
shoulders, well filled in. Long, narrow, well filled
back curving from shoulders to tail.   20

32

Tail — Long, narrow, closely folded, and well curved
under the perch.   5

Style — Well raised up, forming a high circle. Bold,
free and jaunty carriage, plenty of life and action.   25

Size — Approximately 6¾ inches (17cm).   10

Quality and Condition — Clean, healthy, in perfect
condition.   10
                                                                              ───
                                                                              100

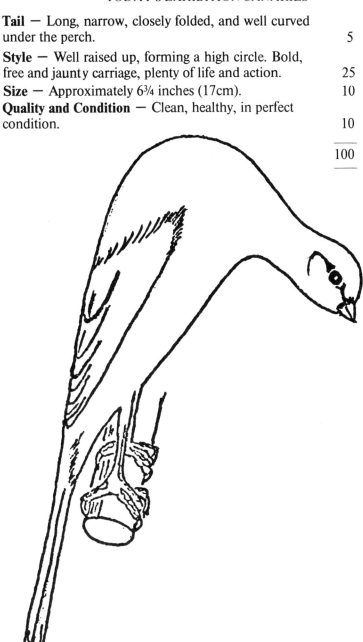

Figure 2.16 The present-day Belgian Fancy model

33

THE BELGIAN CANARY

This variety of canary made its appearance in the U.K. about 1880, and some English breeds in their early days were related to it, such as the Scotch Fancy and the early Yorkshires. Breeding records of it in the U.K. ceased in the early 1900's, but there is still a recorded **Standard of Excellence** kept for it by the **Old Varieties Canary Association.**

THE FIFE FANCY CANARY

This is the latest development of a new **type** canary; as its name implies, it originated in Fife, Scotland, and is one of the smallest canaries. It first appeared in 1952 and is slowly establishing itself on the show bench. The Fife Fancy Canary Club was founded in 1956, since when several area Specialist Clubs have come into being.

Great Oaks from Little Acorns grow

Fifes were exhibited for the first time at the December **National Bird Show** in 1981, and in July 1982, in Australia, received their first recognition on a National basis. No-one can expect a big entry at the National but everything has to start somewhere. Their progress in the U.K. has exceeded expectations. When first given separate classes at the National in 1975 an entry of 50 Fifes was received and it had grown to 190 in 1979. In 1980 there were 253 entries and in 1981 this had risen to 308.

The 1981 entry is even more impressive when you consider that the only other Section to increase their entries over the 1980 figure was the Crests, up two from 48 to 50 entries. The other seven canary sections dropped a combined total of 606 entries. Norwich almost held their own, only dropping 11 from 559 to 548, Yorkshires were down 139 from 448 to 309 (only one ahead of the Fifes), Borders were down 248 from 1,416 to 1,168, Glosters were down 74 from 790 to 716, Coloured Canaries were down 46 from 391 to 345, Lizards were down 62 from 203 to 141 (below Fifes for the second year in succession), and Old Varieties were down 26 from 126 to 100. With only 18 classes, 9 each in Open and Novice and no young bird classes, the Fifes had an average of over 17 entries per class at the 1981 National.

In the U.K., the Border Fancy remains king with the Gloster Fancy the only serious challenger and the Norwich an easy third, but how long the Coloureds and Yorkshires can keep the Fife out of fourth spot only time will tell. In Australia they will need several years for the Fife to become established so the other sections have no immediate worry from the Fife, but with not everyone addicted to size I will be surprised if the Fife does not eventually become as big a force in the Fancy in Australia as it is becoming in the U.K.

34

Figure 2.17 Fife Fancy Canary (Yellow Hen)

Standard

Points

Head — Small, round and neat; beak fine, eye central
to roundness of head and body.   10

Body — Well filled and nicely rounded, running in
almost a straight line from the gentle rise over the
shoulder to the point of the tail, chest also nicely
rounded, but neither heavy or prominent.   10

Wings — Compact and carried close to the body,
meeting at the tips just below root of tail.   10

Legs — Of medium length showing little thigh.   5

Plumage — Close, firm, fine in quality.   10

Tail — Close packed and narrow, being nicely
rounded and filled in at the root.   5

Position — Semi-erect, standing at an angle of 60⁰
Carriage — Gay, jaunty, with full poise of head.   10

Colour — Rich, soft and pure, as level in tint as
possible throughout, but extreme depth and hardness
such as colour feeding gives are debarred.   10

Health — Condition and cleanliness shall have due
weight.   5

Size — Not to exceed 4¼ inches.   25
                                                                       ———
                                                                       100

Open Show
Schedule of Classes

Ch.	Nov.	
243	252	**Clear Yellow or Variegated Cock**
244	253	**Clear Yellow or Variegated Hen**
245	254	**Clear Buff or Variegated Cock**
246	255	**Clear Buff or Variegated Hen**
247	256	**Three Parts Dark, Self or Foul Yellow Cock**
248	257	**Three Parts Dark, Self or Foul Yellow Hen**
249	258	**Three Parts Dark, Self or Foul Buff Cock**
250	259	**Three Parts Dark, Self or Foul Buff Hen**
251	260	**White or Allied to White, Self or Foul, Cock or Hen**

EXTINCT BREEDS

There are several very old and famous varieties of canaries which are now extinct. The following two are perhaps the best known and deserve special comment.

The Lancashire Coppy

This was the largest canary that has ever been bred, being some 9 to 9½ inches (23-24cm) in length, and it had a crest on the top of its head. The first record of it goes as far back as 1760, and for well over a hundred years it was greatly prized in the North of England. It became extinct in 1930, when all today's varieties took over. Efforts are now being made to recreate this old breed, and recreations have appeared in the **Old Variety of Canary.**

36

Figure 2.18 Lancashire Coppy of 1880

Standard

	Points
Head and Coppy	**30**
Neck, Fullness and Thickness	**10**
Back, Round, Full and Long	**10**
Length and Substance	**25**
Upstanding Position and Type	**15**
Condition and Cleanliness	**10**
	100

Figure 2.19 The London Fancy

The London Fancy

This canary's record goes back to 1730; it was a unique canary for the fact that it was a completely clear yellow or buff in colour, except for its tail and flight feathers which were black in colour. These contrasting colours must have made it a very attractive canary. This bird also became extinct in 1930, after slowly losing its popularity during its last fifty years. The reason for this is the fact that some birds were bred with light feathers in the wing or tail. The breeder then either dyed them black or cut the feathers very short. After the bird had been exhibited and often won its class the breeder sold it for a handsome price; when the bird moulted out, the light coloured feathers grew again! This, naturally enough, caused much criticism.

Since 1945 several breeders have tried to reproduce this bird, using a Lizard Canary to produce the black feathers. After spending some years attempting this without any true success, the attempt has failed. Although many attempts have been made to recreate this breed, no real success has been achieved by anyone.

Old Variety Canaries

Open show
Schedule of Classes

EXHIBITORS IN CLASSES 267-270 AND 279-288 MUST STATE COCK OR HEN AND IN CLASSES 285-288 IF UNFLIGHTED ON ENTRY FORM.

267   Lancashire Coppy, Flighted, Cock or Hen
268   Lancashire Coppy, Unflighted, Cock or Hen
269   Lancashire Plainhead, Flighted, Cock or Hen
270   Lancashire Plainhead, Unflighted, Cock or Hen
271   Scotch Fancy, Flighted, Cock
272   Scotch Fancy, Unflighted, Cock
273   Scotch Fancy, Flighted, Hen
274   Scotch Fancy, Unflighted, Hen
275   Parisian Frill, Flighted, Cock
276   Parisian Frill, Unflighted, Cock
277   Parisian Frill, Flighted, Hen
278   Parisian Frill, Unflighted, Hen
279   North or South Dutch Frill, Gibber, Flighted, Cock or Hen
280   North or South Dutch Frill, Gibber, Unflighted, Cock or Hen
281   Belgian, Flighted, Cock or Hen
282   Belgian, Unflighted, Cock or Hen
283   *Any other Old Variety Canary (Hoso, Padovan etc.), Flighted Cock or Hen
284   *Any other Old Variety Canary (Hoso, Padovan etc.), Unflighted Cock or Hen

NOVICE CLASSES

285   Any Scotch Fancy, Cock or Hen
286   Any Frill Canary, Cock or Hen
287   Any Lancashire Canary, Cock or Hen
288   Any Other Old Variety Canary, Cock or Hen

* Please name variety on Entry Form.

CHAPTER 3

Breeding

It is essential to keep records of your breeding results. The value of any records depends upon the information which they contain. In order to be of any value to the breeder they must be accurate. Before the start of the breeding season, you should know certain facts about each bird which you intend to use for breeding purposes, and when the breeding season is over you should have recorded all the necessary facts concerning each youngster you have bred, i.e., type, sex, general appearance and any weakness in the bird's make-up.

Breeders who make a success of their hobby attribute it to a complete thoroughness of method, as well as efficiency, and there must be the same attention to detail in the keeping of records. If a number of breeding pairs are kept, a stud book should be filled in, at the same time as the youngsters are ringed. When the young birds are separated from their parents, a split ring should be used and a record of the ring entered in your stud book, showing the bird's pedigree.

INITIAL PURCHASES

Be very careful when buying your new stock. Great care should be exercised in obtaining good quality birds. It is advisable to get in touch with the secretary of a local society, who is in a position to supply the names of reliable breeders. Do not simply purchase your birds from the first name and address which you find in a year book.

Sources of stock

The purchase of birds from successful exhibitors has greatly increased during the past few years and, this being so, a warning is necessary to newcomers to the Fancy.

Many people visit shows and, by buying birds which have taken awards, reckon that they too will be in the cards with the youngsters they produce. This is often a sorry mistake, as it requires a great deal of knowledge to attain success in this way. It is by no means a general rule that all the exhibitors bred

PAIR (or CAGE) No. ....SEASON ....

Cock	Hen
RING NO	RING NO ....
COLOUR	COLOUR ....
BRED BY	BRED BY ....
SIRE	SIRE ....
....	....
DAM	DAM ....
....	....

DATE SENT SET	NO. OF EGGS	DUE TO HATCH	NO. OF YOUNG	RING NOS. OF YOUNG	DESCRIPTION, PERFORMANCE OR OTHER REMARKS

Figure 3.1 Breeding card; essential for maintaining accurate records

41

the birds that they have had on show. The club secretary may be in a position to advise you on this point. No doubt the best fanciers from whom to purchase new stock are those who strive to breed winners for their own satisfaction. Such people are true fanciers and usually possess good, reliable stock.

However, very good birds are never plentiful. A breeder is very fortunate if he can produce half a dozen high-class birds in a single breeding season, but that, of course, depends on the number of pairs he has put down. It is next to impossible to start at the bottom and reach the top if the breeder's stock is inferior. **I would impress upon the keen beginner the absolute necessity of buying the best that his pocket allows.** Such purchases should be made from fanciers who are not just in the hobby to make money.

Recommended type

It is usually found that the progeny of medium sized birds is more even and the points better balanced than in the case of youngsters bred from a large cock and a small hen, or from a large hen and a small cock. If you cannot obtain two birds of a medium size, have plenty of size in the cock with good, deep colour and a good, round, broad, clean skull free from browiness. The hen should have good type and quality of feather. Normally you will find type will come from the hen and that size and colour derive from the cock.

Furthermore, I would be against the novice attempting to breed double-Buff or double-Yellow. It is better to start in the orthodox manner by pairing Yellow to Buff or Buff to Yellow until you have gained some experience of your stock. This is the accepted way to breed Borders, for example, and is quite possibly one of the main reasons why Borders are one of the very few varieties of canary which are free from lumps or feather cysts.

TWO BUFFS

If you find that your birds are becoming deficient in size or feather quality, you may then pair together two Buffs. In doing so, **always use birds with a fine feather.** On no account use Buffs which are rough in feather, as this undesirable quality is very easily transmitted and birds of this appearance have little chance on the show bench when in good competition.

By mating two Buffs you will increase the size of your birds and probably the feather quality at the same time. In double-Buffing great care must be exercised, or the birds will become too big and rough in feather.

When breeding with a view to producing first-class show birds, it is best to have a definite breeding plan in mind. First, breed only from the best quality stock.

Inbreeding

On the question of inbreeding a great deal has been written. One is told of the advantageous policy of accumulating all the tendencies or characteristics transmitted to the young birds. The ordinary breeder will soon see difficulties. The first is that it is impossible to follow such a methodical system without considerable line-breeding. However, it is also true that a breeder who is constantly buying in stock for crossing purposes will never establish a good line in his own stock. He is constantly introducing hereditary tendencies which he knows very little about and which turn up in the young unexpectedly. It must be remembered that every variety has points which demand patience to acquire.

PATIENCE DEMANDED

A breeder cannot expect to make any headway with his stock if he makes a practice of selling all his best birds. You cannot have both the money from selling your birds and retain your essential stock at the same time. In my opinion, the birds come first.

It has been mentioned that in pairing the general rule is Yellow x Buff. It is immaterial which is the cock. The object is to produce young birds of good feathering. The Buffs supply the close compact feather and the Yellows the silkiness of texture and colour. This is only a general rule and one departed from when specific results are required. If a particular strain (good in all other points) has become too finely feathered as a result of inbreeding, it is advisable to pair two Buffs or two Yellows together to counteract this tendency.

Two generations

This procedure may be necessary for one or two generations, until the required feather texture has been obtained, but care should be taken.

There may be other cases for such pairings. It must be understood that the rule applied to feathering is that **the pairing of two Yellows induces thinness and that the pairing of two Buffs has the opposite effect.** The pairing of Yellows and Buffs also affects colour materially. Yellow is the foundation of colour and good birds frequently display it in great purity, yet the tendency of an ordinary Buff is quite the opposite. This is the reason for pairing together two Yellows, being nothing more than a case of one Yellow gene which, in theory, should produce as much colour as that from using two genes. Occasionally it is found necessary to do this because of a peculiar feature in the colour of the feather, due to too much concentration of Buff blood at some previous stage, by which the brilliancy of the yellow has been clouded by a leaning towards a duller shade.

In a case of this kind, the offspring from two Yellows should restore the correct colour. Two Buffs which had been bred from a double-Yellow pairing would have the same impact.

BREEDING HINTS

Breeders often adopt different methods in an effort to obtain results, when experience would tell them to stop. A breeder of high-class canaries should not be without a Green bird in his birdroom; not the dull, flat, smoky Buff Green that one often sees, but a brilliant Yellow Green, which is a beautiful bird. In the event of failing to obtain a bird of this kind, the best alternative is a brilliant Clear Yellow cock. A Variegated Green should show the actual green in its variegation and not brown.

Satisfactory results have sometimes been obtained from first-year hens paired with two or three-year-old cocks, provided, of course, that both birds are healthy and in breeding condition. Young cocks are naturally more vigorous than older ones and the same applies to hens. However, young cocks may display an over-abundance of energy and fail in their prime purpose.

Experienced cock

If a cock has been used for breeding purposes for one or two seasons, and proves to be a good parent, it will teach the young hen her duties towards her family. I have seen an experienced cock collect a supply of eggfood for the hen as soon as the first egg has hatched. After disgorging part of the food into the hen's beak, he should start to feed the youngsters in the nest. While some hens take their parental duties as soon as their partner has supplied them with food, others keep a watchful eye on their mate and feed the youngsters only when he is feeding from the softfood dish.

If a cock pays little attention to the young and allows the hen to feed them entirely on her own, he should be removed from the breeding cage for about 10 days. He can then be returned to the hen so that the next round of eggs will be fertile.

Lack of eggfood

There are some birds which feed their young on hard seed and scarcely any eggfood is taken. This often results in the youngsters dying with their crops full of undigested food.

When you find hens feeding in this manner, give them soaked seed and softfood and try removing their seed hoppers. You must keep an eye on the youngsters, and, if they are not being fed properly, transfer them to another hen who is a reliable feeder.

Inadequate hens

Hens which do not attend to their young because of nervousness or some bodily ailment should be given a variety of food, such as a little crushed hemp, soaked rape or teazle, and a little chickweed. In addition, a bath of weak salt water can be provided for several days and this treatment should restore the birds to full health, so that they can carry out their parental duties.

However, if they still refuse to become good mothers, I would advise breeders to discard these particular hens for breeding purposes. You simply cannot afford to be sentimental when it comes to breeding good quality birds.

Old and young birds

One excellent way of distinguishing an old bird from a young one is by examining the legs. Those of young birds are quite free from scales and the skin looks soft and smooth, but on the more mature, individual scales can be seen forming. It is also usual to find that the young birds' feet are cleaner than those of older ones. Another unmistakeable sign to a practised eye is the greater amount of energy which is shown by the youngsters.

Sexing

A question which is often asked is; how do you tell a cock from a hen? Although there is no certain method going just by appearance, generally a cock has a bolder carriage than the hen, his posture is more erect, his appearance more spruce and he will be more lively in his actions.

As a rule, the cock's head is larger and fuller than the hen's and his plumage is richer, with more depth of colour. The notes of the cock bird are deeper in tone, more mellow and stronger than those of the hen. Another way to distinguish the sex of healthy birds, especially during the spring, is by handling them and examining their vents by blowing away the feathers beneath the tail; the vent of the cock bird protrudes, while that of a hen is broad and flat.

Pairing up

The judgement of when to pair up your birds is the key note to success in the raising of healthy chicks. Although, as a rule, it is safe to assume that like produces like, you must take into account the state of health and appearance of the parents and the grandparents and for this purpose you must go back several generations. It cannot be stressed too often that **a bird with any weakness in form or constitution should not be used for breeding purposes,** as it is far easier to perpetuate flaws than transmit good qualities. In other words, it is easier to breed faults into your birds than to breed in a lasting good feature.

A first indication as to the birds coming into breeding season is when you see the cock feeding the hen. Canaries are among those birds which feed from the crop. The pair are then placed together and they should be supplied with a little softfood and a little soaked seed. The cock will display a rapid fluttering of the wings, accompanied by a twittering note. He will constantly feed the hen by disgorging the contents of his crop. In addition to the eggfood, give a little watercress as well as a little freshly grown rape foliage. This will make him all the more keen to keep the hen supplied with food.

Figure 3.2 Nest pans; *left* wooden variety,
right earthenware type with a gripping rim

Nest building
In the meantime, the hen should be showing signs of wanting to go to nest. Once she reaches this stage, a nest-pan should be supplied and the hen will be seen to enter it, scuffling with her feet and wings to adapt it for her use. At this point the nesting material should be supplied. However, give it only sparingly until she begins to build in earnest, as if given in unlimited quantities it will undoubtedly be wasted. As long as there is nesting material between the wires of the cage the hen will continue to pull it and scatter it about.

When the hen begins in earnest to build her nest, be certain to remove all the soiled nesting material and give her a fresh supply. In the course of a day or two the hen will be taking a beakful of nesting material to the nest-pan. This will continue until the nest is finished to her satisfaction. There will be no alteration to the state of the nest for a day or two. By that time the hen will have become more sedate and will be showing indications of wanting to lay.

Nest-pan
After placing the breeding pair together, it is wise to wait about a week before installing the nest-pan. This breathing space will allow you to see if the birds agree and are likely to make congenial partners. When it is time to install the nest-pan it should be fixed by means of a screw on the side of the cage or by means of some form of support on the base of the cage, although it must be raised up from the floor.

Nest-pans can be placed in either or both ends of the cage. Always place your nest-pan close to the perches and reasonably near to the cage front. Avoid having to lift it down for inspection. A piece of cardboard can be placed on the wire of the cage to give the hen a sense of privacy. The question of leaving the cock with the hen after mating is a tricky one and one must be guided by individual circumstances. There are a large number of breeders who separate the sexes after mating has taken place, but others find that some hens will not sit without the cock. However, these are in the minority.

Interference by the cock

If the cock interferes with her tail feathers or annoys the hen in any way while she is sitting, it is advisable to remove him until the young birds are about 10 days old, when he should then assist the hen to feed them in the normal way. When the eggs have hatched some hens will call the cock bird to feed them on the nest and will not feed the youngsters at all. In this case remove the cock, and she will then have to leave the nest in order to feed. When she returns to the nest she will probably feed the youngsters. However, do not trust her entirely. Keep a sharp lookout and, if necessary, remove the young to a pair of reliable feeders.

Laying difficulties

Sometimes a day before the hen lays she will be seen in the morning to be in the best of health, but by afternoon she will seek a corner of the cage and squat on the floor with her wings outstretched, her feathers ruffled up and her eyes closed. In such a case she should be placed in a hospital cage at a temperature of 25^0 C (77^0 F) and left overnight. When you look at her the next morning you will usually find that she has laid and she can then be returned to her breeding cage.

Red mite

From the time you set the hen on her clutch, you must make special provision to check for red mite. Before you place the eggs under the hen, lift up the nest lining and sprinkle the bottom of the nest-pan with an insect powder, and replace the lining and the eggs.

You will find the hen will now be able to sit in comfort. This method will keep these pests in check. When a hen is troubled with red mite, she becomes restless on the nest and, in preening her feathers in search of the pests, will often break an egg, or dead-in-shell may even result due to the eggs not being kept at the correct temperature. Red mite can easily be detected by the presence of a fine white floury substance beneath the nesting material or under the nest-pan. On close examination it will be found to be alive. Another indication of their presence are the minute white specks dotted along the cross-bar of the cage, or in any crevice along the top of the cage.

Remedy

If these settlements of red mite are left undisturbed they will increase at an alarming rate. Whenever you see any of these signs, spray them with insect powder and if this is done about three times a week you will not be troubled. I find this the best remedy of all. It will also dispose of any grey lice which live on the bodies of the parent birds.

Red mite, unlike grey lice, hide in the daytime and attack at night. If you examine the cage at night with a torch you will see them running over the bird with extraordinary speed. Not only are they troublesome and irritating to the breeding hen but they will also attack the young birds in the nests and suck their blood. I know of several cases of this and, after use of insect powder, there was no more trouble. If you wish to have strong, healthy birds, **keep them free from lice of any kind.**

Canary breeders in southern Europe, who use all-wire cages, do not appear to be as affected by red mite. On the other hand their birds do contract canary pox, as a result of being bitten by mosquitoes. To counteract this, some fanciers vaccinate their canaries on the thighs and such treatment would appear to be quite successful.

In Spain, for example, canaries are bred on open balconies. It is quite impossible to erect a mosquito screen on a narrow balcony as it is also required to dry the family washing, and it is a place of safety for children to play.

The problem of mosquitoes during the canary breeding season also applies to some parts of Australia, but in that country it is a problem that can effectively be controlled.

Overheating

When the hens are sitting during the breeding season, they are liable to become too hot. Great benefit can be derived by giving them a quarter of a teaspoonful of liquid magnesium to the ordinary sized drinking cup of water. If treatment was effected more often while the hens were incubating one would hear of fewer egg-bound hens.

Canary fanciers in the Mediterranean area use all-wire breeding and stock cages. Although the temperature is for several months at a time well in excess of 100° F (38^{0} C) in the shade, generally speaking there are few cases of dead-in-shell. In the United Kingdom we often blame too dry an atmosphere for causing dead-in-shell. Personally, I do not agree with this. In my opinion dead-in-shell is more likely to be caused when the eggs are not maintained at the right incubation temperature. This year, when I kept a cock and hen together for the whole of the breeding season, I did not have a single case of dead-in-shell. One very interesting observation was that whenever the sitting hen left the nest, the cock bird took over the task of incubating the eggs until his mate returned.

In the countries with hot, dry, summers which I have visited, after talking to many local fanciers, it would appear that their birds produce more clear eggs than we record in our birdrooms. I think that the reason for this is the fact that they have a much shorter spring in which their canaries can come into a more gradual and natural breeding condition. There is a moral here for us. Do not try to force either your cocks or your hens into breeding condition. Just simply feed them a good, balanced diet, ensure that the birdroom is draught-free, and then leave the rest to nature. Fifty years ago, the modern craze of early breeding with canaries and with budgerigars did not exist. In those days the breeding season commenced when the birds had reached that natural condition in either April or May.

Incubation

As the laying period is spread over five days, it is evident that the first egg will be hatched three days before the fourth one, with the result that the oldest chick will be the strongest, and more likely to receive a greater share of the food at the expense of its nest-mates.

This unfair position can be avoided by removing the first three eggs from the nest with a spoon as they are laid and replacing them with dummies. Gently remove the hen from the nest and carefully exchange the eggs. It is sometimes worthwhile to warm the dummy eggs slightly with a fidgety hen as she will recognise the difference in the temperatures of the eggs. The good egg is placed in a small box partly filled with bran. Be sure to turn the eggs twice a day.

BREEDING FAULTS

Let us now consider those things which detract from the ideal type of canary which is common to all type canaries. These, of course, can be many, some are inherited and permanent, and some can even be corrected by proper management.

Porportion

It is very important that, in all the different types of canaries, the head and shoulders are in proportion to the body. This is particularly noticeable in Borders where many otherwise excellent quality birds just fail to have that all important nip in the neck before joining the body.

I personally advise all breeders to concentrate on breeding canaries which excel for type, are vivacious and attractive to the eye, and not a bird which has exaggerated length or size of body. If we were breeding chickens for the table it would, of course, be completely different, but we are not, so where show points are essential we must relegate mere size. **A bird which is in excellent proportion will beat the larger but less well proportioned bird every time.** If you attempt to enlarge a bird to above the average size, you will only produce a disproportion between the head and body; at the same time you will increase the coarseness of feather and with it loss of its all-round quality.

In some breeds I have no fault to find with a big well-proportioned bird

Figure 3.3 Faults in a Border Fancy; *(a)* position on perch *(b)* long flighted

which has excellent colouring and good carriage, thus creating the impression of grace and general symmetry which is so necessary in a show bird. It is, however, very necessary that we first produce these features in the smaller, more typical birds; we should always encourage show points and not discourage it just for being a smaller bird.

The lack of proportion in a canary is, therefore, probably the most noticeable fault to anyone with an experienced eye. I find that many breeders'

Figure 3.4 Gloster Corona fault; split in crest

birds fail through poor carriage; the failure of a canary to display itself properly at the time that it is judged can often be the reason why we sometimes see an excellent bird placed second in its class. That is why it is so vitally essential that we note all the defects in our breeding records. No fancier ever produces a **Best Canary in Show** if he allows sentiment to rule his better judgement when selecting breeding pairs.

Shape

As an incorrect shape is all too frequently also seen in a bird which has incorrect carriage, and as symmetry, proportion, and carriage are so dependent on the bird having the correct position, I cannot stress too strongly just how important it is to remember this when selecting your breeding pairs. Lack of attention to this is the reason why so many fanciers take many different breeding seasons before they can see an improvement in the type and quality of their birds.

51

Figure 3.5 Norwich fault; narrow, mean, and flat above the beak

Always remember that with a canary the beauty of type can be enhanced or marred by the bird's actual carriage, and type is so dependent on its complete make-up, i.e. head, neck, body, tail and legs. It really is a most difficult thing to get to the ideal but, when you have actually bred a bird which closely resembles the ideal, then what a feeling of achievement you have.

COLOUR FAULTS IN GREENS

To breed a really good green canary is a most difficult thing to achieve. First, let us decide just what shade of green we are trying to produce; most fanciers will say a **grass** green. Now there are many different grasses, most of which have their own particular shade of green; personally, I always describe a yellow green canary as having the same shade of green as that of the outside of a young holly leaf, and a buff green canary as having the same shade of green as the underside of the young holly leaf.

Experienced breeders of green canaries say that it is easier to breed a small canary which excels in depth of colour and, of course, they are quite right. The difference between a small canary and a large one is, generally speaking, a matter of the size of its feather; a small bird has a finer feather which readily shows its natural colour, a larger bird has a larger and more coarse feather; hence the same depth of colour is now on a large, open, coarse feather and the bird loses its true depth of colour.

I would like to say something about show points; this is something which is inherent in the make-up of a particular canary and is something which is capable of being passed on from parent to its young, that is why I say that **type** is given by the hen. I like all my breeding hens to be good for type and to look their sex.

HIDDEN FACTORS

The visible quality of a canary is most important except for actual size, which is not so important. There may be hidden factors which could detract from the quality of the breeding pair and these can only be brought to light through breeding. This is where line breeding through a bird's genes will bring out the defects as well as the good points. You could compare the use of genes as well as line breeding as the true reason why some fanciers' show teams consistently remain at the forefront of their variety.

By consistently continuing to line breed, the resulting young, through their genes, will show their undesirable features as well as those which you are trying to breed into your own stock. Those young ones which do not show any undesirable features should be used for breeding purposes as this will then show if they are carrying any recessive undesirable features, in which case they must be discarded because these birds are the carriers of the genes which you are trying to suppress. If none appear in some of the young then these birds can become the foundation of a very successful stud. If one of these birds happens to be a cock, then he should be paired to two closely related hens which have no visible defects. Should one of his hens produce a number of third-rate birds, then the hen and all her young ones should be disposed of.

This process of analysis of a bird's 'unknown' will show up just where the adverse genes are being created; the genes have been given the opportunity to get together by line breeding and we can see how important this progeny testing is.

SHOW FEATURES AND BREEDING CAPACITY

We often talk of a bird's outstanding show features and that particular bird's ability to reproduce them; this, of course, will depend on its background ancestry, and also whether it is genetically suited to its partner. Much also will depend upon you pairing up the birds as they reach their peak of breeding condition — a half-fit bird will never breed a dominant bird of outstanding type.

Now let us look at the difference between a big bold cock and one that is smaller but equally active. It does not necessarily follow that a cock that is big and bold is also strong bodily, in which case he has less to pass on to his young. Mere size can be misleading as this could quite easily be due to the size of the bird's feather. Personally, I prefer a cock bird of average size which is good for type, has the correct length of leg, is vigorous, has a clear visible round eye, and good quality of feather which shows its full colour.

With a hen the first consideration is type. Another desirable feature is a nice quality of feather, and she **must** be a genuinely active bird who uses her flight cage and actively searches for food. These types of hen as a rule make the best parents, and are least likely to become egg-bound.

Now let us consider for a moment the head qualities of our pair of birds; here an experienced eye not only picks out their head qualities but also their breeding capacity. Personally, I do not favour a hen which has the head qualities of a cock, they are generally less dependable as breeders. I much prefer that each bird visibly displays its sex; I am, of course, quite well aware of the fact that the Standard of Excellence in every variety applies to both cocks and hens.

When selecting your breeding pair, if the hen closely resembles that as laid down in the Standard of Excellence, then you are on the right road to success. If I am selecting a hen to act as a feeder, I look for one which readily shows its sex, has a good clear eye, and is active in its ways and habits.

POINTS TO AVOID

With a hen which naturally lacks that little extra depth in the pelvis in the area where the legs join the body, a careful watch should be kept when she is due to lay for egg binding; needless to say, where a hen produces large-sized eggs there is always a greater possibility of egg binding occurring.

THE REASON FOR FAILURE

I know of fanciers who have had success after success every year and then I note that, over a couple of show seasons, they produce very few class winners at the major shows, although their general standard is high. The reason for this is the fact that their successful rivals are breeding more young birds which are carrying the double factor, so that the original fancier has no alternative but to bring into his stock some of these double factor birds. Failure to do so will only result in a continued decline in the overall quality of his birds.

Whilst the **Standard of Excellence** as laid down for our particular variety is fixed, a successful exhibitor must always be ahead of the standard achieved by the present-day winners. It is the all important quality of the birds which counts, and we should always look for an all-round improvement as it becomes difficult to discriminate between many good birds; always look for one feature capable of improvement, as is incorporated in the **standard.**

Let us presume that the feature that you are looking for is wing carriage. You have been winning well with birds which are very good for type, until one show season you find your birds second or third in their class at a show, and the winning birds have the same type as yours, the difference being in the wing carriage. Then, at the next breeding season, when you are selecting your breeding pairs, ensure that you bring into your stock a similar **type** of bird, which excels in wing carriage. Then a fair percentage of the young which they will have bred should be class winners themselves, and you will be back again to your winning ways.

We should always remember that it is very doubtful if any bird is pure for all the genes which are desired to breed the perfect **type** and supposing one such bird was bred, money would not be able to buy it. You will have a much better chance of obtaining a bird which is outstanding for the point that you are looking for if you are prepared to accept one which is slightly lacking in some respect in which your own birds excel.

The actual selection quality of your breeding stock depends on two things which **you** personally must have:

1. A well trained eye which gives you the ability to **select** the right stock; this is one thing which you **must** cultivate.

2. Having achieved that, then your brain must know which two birds are to be paired together.

The successful fancier does not have a birdroom full of excellent stock solely because of their excellence, half of the reason for his success is because he has acquired the ability to select successful breeding pairs. So before condemning your breeding stock for not producing quality young ones, you must examine your judgement of the breeding pairs.

FEEDING

Some canary fanciers have difficulty in keeping their stock in really top condition irrespective of the time of the year. The result is that, when the all important breeding season comes along, their birds are just not in a naturally fit breeding condition. Very often this is the result of the breeder not having fed his stock a natural and fully balanced diet. It might even be that the environment of the birdroom is not right through bad hygiene, lack of fresh air, or the birdroom windows facing the wrong way.

Figure 3.6 Sow thistle; very good to give feeding hens

Perhaps the fancier has failed to realise just how easily bacteria and diseases are transmitted by the cage drinker. It is always advisable to use a drinker which is difficult for the birds to foul, or in which fouled shavings cannot easily fall. Personally, I always try to make a point of changing the drinking water twice a day. Most Australian fanciers, I noticed, used a drip bottle type drinker which, in fact, is like a small medicine bottle on which has been fastened a salt-cellar top; perhaps if we were to enjoy their summer weather we, too, would do the same!

Multi-vitamins

As an aid to a canary's general good health, and to keep them in this condition, I suggest putting a multi-vitamin preparation in their drinking water. A very successful canary breeder friend of mine gives his birds **Orovite '7'** vitamin powder solution mixed with their drinking water. With this particular solution, the thing to appreciate is the fact that a Novice could not accidentally feed it to his stock, as a canary's digestive system will only absorb the amount of **Orovite '7'** it requires; any surplus vitamin given to the bird is disposed of through the bird's droppings. You can obtain **Orovite '7'** from Boots the Chemists.

Seed

The basic diet of a canary is, of course, canary seed, but it is necessary to ensure that it has matured naturally while growing. When fresh, good quality canary seed is opened by removing the husk. The kernel inside will be found to be a rich walnut brown colour; the outer shell of such seed is a pale gold colour, with a clean, bright appearance. Dull looking seed will always open up with a very light, or a very dark looking skin, this is the sign of a bad harvesting or artificial drying. Always take a critical look at canary seed when buying it. Never consistently feed your canaries on a too richly balanced seed diet, for this could lead to kidney complaints.

Eggfood

Like most Australian canary fanciers I advocate the use of eggfood all the year round, but I am careful to adjust its composition to the season of the year. When the birds are not breeding I greatly reduce the amount of hard-boiled egg and glucose content, and the number of times a week that it is fed to my stock as well as the quantity per bird.

Rape seed

This oily type of seed is one of the cabbage family; most leading authorities on seeds use it as a bird food, all generally agree that **German Summer Rape** is by far the best. Most leading fanciers that I know use red rape mixed with their canary seed and most Roller fanciers have great faith in it.

For those fanciers who keep colour fed type canaries, I suggest that they feed rape seed separately before and during the moulting season. At that time it should be crushed and then lightly sprinkled with colour food, similar to when it is mixed with softfood; many Continental fanciers who have New Colour Canaries do this.

Greenfood

To ensure that your birds enjoy a balanced diet of vitamins it is essential that they have a supply of various natural greenfood to supplement the vitamins which are deficient in the seed, the supply of which will naturally depend on the time of year. I suggest a mixture of the following: dandelion, watercress, sprouts, cabbage, chickweed, both the seeding heads and tender leaves and roots cut open of seeding dandelion, seeding spinach, green succulent seeding dock, seeding thistle heads, and short seeding light green grasses which grow under trees. All birds feed best on a mixture of seeds and greenfood. If you have a spare few yards in your garden then you should sow a cup of rape seeds in early September which should be lightly raked into the soil. By the time that you have young canaries in the nest, the rape plant will be full of yellow flowers which the feeding hens will greatly enjoy feeding to their young, who in turn will thrive on it, and you will easily be able to see

Figure 3.8 Seeding dock

Figure 3.7 Chickweed

their rate of growth. When the flowers are over then give the feeding hens the young rape plant's tender green leaves, which you will find are enjoyed almost as much as the flowers.

In a **fresh** condition it makes good deficiences of calcium, iron, iodine, and manganese. The basic cause of digestive disorders is generally a lack of greenfood, which must only be fed while it is fresh and certain essential amino acids and vitamins, as well as many different trace elements, are present.

The fibre in greenfood is essential for proper digestion in birds living on shelled seed, because the digestive bacteria produce vitamins and fibre which results in better digestion. You will find that feeding hens which are given plenty of greenfood produce young excellent in feather growth and quality of finish.

You should also try growing for your canaries chicory, silver beet and Chinese cabbage. When you first start to feed your birds any greenfood additional to what they normally have, it should be fed in small quantities until the birds' systems have got used to it. I do **not** recommend that you start feeding your hens, who have young in the nest, a new, completely unfamiliar greenfood. You will probably have noticed that I have not mentioned the use of lettuce; personally, I never use it as I consider it very overrated, besides having a very high water content, which for young birds under ten days old can be detrimental as it has a very purging effect on them. Lettuce contains approximately 95% water. A **small** piece of crisp lettuce could be fed to birds on a hot summer's day when they are approaching their nest feather moult.

DIET

It is not known how little of a given artificial constituent is necessary to maintain good health and, while it is known that the body can absorb only a certain amount of a given constituent, the excess passing through the body unabsorbed, it is also unknown what the maximum is; the motto should be 'little and not too often'.

As long as a bird's diet supplies **energy, heat** and **body building constituents,** plus other substances containing vitamins, all appears to be well. In other words, we supply our birds with a good mixed diet then judge the results of our efforts by observing the bird's general health, its capability during the breeding season, its freedom from disease and its life span. In an endeavour to assist you in this sphere, I trust that this will be of help.

Food has three main functions:

(a) To provide heat and energy;

(b) To provide material to build, or renew, body tissues;

(c) To regulate body processes.

For many years a great deal of attention was paid to the first two functions, and any diet which provided these was regarded as adequate. It is only in latter years that the vast number of dietary factors required to regulate body processes has been recognised.

Essential constituents of food

Besides oxygen and water the body requires the following:

    (a) Proteins;

    (b) Carbohydrates;

    (c) Fats;

    (d) Mineral Salts;

    (e) Vitamins.

Proteins

These are the builders of body tissue. They are required to build new tissue and for replacing the loss which occurs through daily wear and tear.

Carbohydrates

These include various starches and sugars which supply energy to the body. Most carbohydrates are broken down by the digestive juices to form glucose and eventually burned up to form carbon dioxide and water. Should more carbohydrates than are required for immediate energy be eaten, they are converted into fat and stored in the body tissues.

Fats

These are also energy-providing food. Fats vary in quality according to the amount of vitamin 'A' and 'D' that they contain.

Mineral Salts

The body requires many different mineral elements, including iron, calcium, phosphorus, iodine, copper and potassium. Normally, a good varied diet would provide the necessary minerals, but young growing birds require additional minerals such as an iron tonic. This is also necessary with adult birds during the moulting period.

The chief sources of iron are liver extract, egg yolk, wheat germ and green vegetables. Small pieces of rock salt which have been soaked in water for five minutes, will readily be licked dry by the birds that it is given to. Do not forget to give all your birds an adequate supply of cuttlefish bone, it provides all the calcium that the birds require.

Vitamins

These are essential and cannot be manufactured in the body, they can only be provided by feeding a balanced diet. I personally know just how beneficial Orovite '7' vitamin powder can be when given to canaries in their drinking water. All greenfood should be fed to the birds while **fresh,** otherwise much of its food value will be lost.

Softfood

Some fanciers favouring natural-coloured birds tend to discontinue the use of softfood when they see the chicks de-husking and eating hard seed. This is wrong, for the chicks' crops and stomachs are **not** fully developed and are very tender. With that in mind, they should be given the ration of softfood right through the moult. It will help to keep them fit and well, and will certainly stop the so-called 'going light' trouble which is nothing more than chronic indigestion.

Feeding during the moult

During the moult, feeding can enhance the basic colour of canaries. We should always remember that nature herself provides the best food to increase the depth of the bird's natural colour, and that is why birds in the wild have such richly coloured feathers.

For breeders of colour-fed canaries, do not neglect to feed your normal colour food at the same time as you are endeavouring to bring out your birds' **natural** colour; this must be commenced a month before they start to moult. Do not forget that during the moulting period natural foods such as chickweed, sow thistle, shepherd's purse, green seeding dock and seeding grasses, can all be found in abundance in fields, allotments, parks and gardens. These should all be collected and fed fresh to the birds. Some foods, such as plantain when ripe, can be collected, put in paper bags to keep out the dust — first making sure that they are **dry** and will not go musty — and fed throughout the winter, much to the birds' delight. **Always ensure that your wild seeds have not been sprayed with any insecticide or weed killer.**

Those who live in a large city and do not have access to nature's own supply of seeds, can go to a good greengrocer and obtain spinach, cabbage, brussel sprouts, chicory, watercress, and so on. The common marigold is also used by many Australians as well as nasturtium leaves. Such foods will help to enhance the natural ground colour of the canaries.

During the moult, Parrish's Chemical Food is a good tonic for the birds; it should be added to their drinking water, two or three times a week. Some breeders, however, put it in the softfood. Care should be taken to ensure that it is not over-fed, because if it is, the birds will develop a distinct pinkish hue which can spoil their colour. It has been found that Cod Liver Oil used in excess during the moult tends to bleach the colour.

Mixed seed for the breeding season

During the breeding season I am a firm believer in feeding sprouted mixed seed which is made up of 25% **teazle,** as now described. First mix your seed well together, and put it in a jar not more than two-thirds full, as the seed will swell with soaking. Next, fill the jar with boiling water, and with a fork gently stir the seed in the water. Leave it soaking for twenty-four hours, put all the soaked seed in a large sieve, then put it under a strongly running cold water tap for at least five minutes. This is to remove all bacteria. Leave it to drain off for twelve hours, then put all the soaked seed in a plastic bag, and tie up the top of the bag. With the aid of a fork, pierce the bag well above the seed, to give ventilation, and leave it in the airing cupboard for three days. By now the seed will have commenced to sprout, and its vitamin content will have more than doubled. You can now safely give it to your feeding hens, and the chicks in the nest will thrive on it.

Sprouted seed

This last breeding season saw a very definite lack of seeding chickweed when the first round young birds came along. A Norwich breeder I know by mid-May had already bred some 30 youngsters, and he had fed his stock sprouted seed and not chickweed.

After soaking his seed, he was very careful to rinse it thoroughly in cold water and allow a period of 12 hours for the surplus to drain off the seed before placing it in a plastic bag.

After this he put it in a cupboard for three days while the seed commenced to sprout. The lack of this sprouted seed could be the reason for the death of some of the young birds in the nest.

OTHER BREEDING PREPARATIONS

In February, I collect all my earthenware nest-pans together and then, with the aid of a one inch brush, I generously paint the inside of them with an anti-mite solution and then leave them to dry for a month. The next job is to sew the nest lining inside them. For nesting material I use carpet **non**-fibrous underfelt which has been washed and dried thoroughly the previous summer. I also make the nest linings from it. By painting the insides of my nest-pans, and using really clean linings and nesting material, I never get any kind of mite in the nests. The only mite trouble which occurs from time to time is that which is present on chickweed which, when put in a breeding cage, very quickly infests the nest of chicks. When this happens I sprinkle the nest, and under the chicks, with Keating's Powder. In less than two hours the mites are dead, and the hen has not interrupted her feeding activities.

During the actual breeding and especially the rearing of the young ones in the nest, the parents adopt almost automatically the diet of a softbill bird. You will find that the cage seed hopper will only require to be topped up once a week. The wild canary in its natural habitat, during the breeding season, lives entirely on young green succulent seeding grasses and, under these conditions, they are quite prolific breeders. This is something which supports my suggestion of supplying sprouted seed to feeding canaries. At this time of

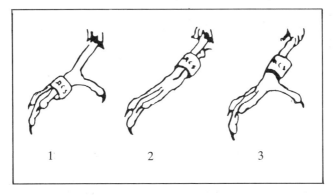

Figure 3.9 Ringing. 1, Holding the bird on its back in your left hand, pass the ring over the front claws with your right hand. 2, Pass the ring over the hind claw. 3, Allow the hind claw to come back into position. The ring is now safely on the leg

Figure 3.10 Wooden Nest Pan (used in UK only)

the year it is important that you continue giving your birds granulated charcoal.

For the less experienced breeder it is recommended that you breed from actual pairs of birds, and do not run one cock with two or three hens. It is always nice to see, when a sitting hen leaves her nest to take a little exercise and a quick feed, how most cocks will actually go and sit in the nest.

Ringing your birds
All who breed canaries should adopt the practice of ringing their chicks with closed club rings. This provides a check for the breeder and gives him a constant record of a bird's history. To do this, turn the bird on its back in your left hand, and with the right hand pass the ring over the front claws, up the leg and over the hind claw, which is then allowed to come back into position. The ring will then be safely on the leg. The usual age for ringing the birds is five to seven days. It is most important to check each chick for a few days after ringing to make sure the ring has not slipped off.

Nest boxes
Some fanciers use a square shaped nest box which has a gauze type bottom; in these cases the nest box fixing bracket should be hung from behind the head of a screw secured to either the side or back of the cage. The nest box should be so made as to allow a ¾ inch gap between the cage and the nest box; this should remove the possibility of the cage paintwork being soiled when the young birds void over the side of the nest pan.

ONE ROUND ONLY

A friend of mine who is a very successful Border exhibitor uses approximately 18 hens and slightly fewer cocks. He takes one round from each hen, and never pairs up his birds until the latter part of April. Other interesting points are the fact that 75 per cent of his breeding hens are unflighted birds and that he often disposes of half of his breeding stock by the end of June.

CHAPTER 4

Breeding Stock, Genetics and Colour

In this chapter, amongst other subjects, I would like to express a few words about the gulf which exists between the average breeder and the geneticist; this is, I think, partly due to the language which the latter choose to use. To explain it in everyday usage, the geneticist is only really trying to explain the principles of Mendel as regards colour reproduction, and I have no intention of talking about the subject in highly technical terms so, as we progress through this chapter, I will endeavour to talk in non-technical terms while explaining my point.

PAIRING

There is always controversy over the best time to pair the birds, but to be on the safe side I always advise waiting until the beginning of spring. Some breeders start earlier than this, being willing to risk the hen becoming egg-bound, should there be a sudden cold night. If this trouble occurs, it may be with a hen you greatly prize. As well as causing you many an anxious thought during the period of treatment, it will probably impair her breeding powers for the whole season.

Stock selection

In the selection of stock, the age of the bird is immaterial. Buy good quality birds and never mind their age, so long as they are healthy. A 12-month-old bird still carries a fair proportion of its nest feathering, especially on the wings and tail. However, it is said to be a mature bird.

The cocks will watch out eagerly for mates. The hens will be equally anxious to commence their duties and, if left by themselves, will lay nests of infertile eggs and sit on them. I have never found that age made any difference to successful breeding, or that young birds lacked any knowledge in the art of reproduction. However, in this anxiety to exercise their natural instinct there is need for caution. During the breeding season, you must resist the temptation to put the birds together before they are fit for the task ahead of them.

65

Points to watch

It is very foolish to start with more birds than you can give sufficient attention to, as if you are forced to neglect the necessary treatment, due to lack of time or for any other reason, you are almost sure of disappointing results.

Birds bred from parents in which one or both are affected with asthma or any other disease, never become healthy, bright birds, and remain miserable-looking specimens which spoil the appearance of your birdroom. Some die during their first moult. If the cock is more in breeding condition than the hen with which he has mated, the birds will be continually fighting each other. This is a most important point often neglected by beginners, as well as seasoned fanciers. Even after some experience in the art of breeding, it is sometimes advisable to keep new birds out of your birdroom until you are satisfied that they are free from any disability or infection. In other words, they should be placed in quarantine.

Preparing for breeding

After the moult and just before the start of the winter, both sexes should be housed in separate, large flight cages. By about December the fancier should have decided upon the birds from which he is going to breed during the coming season. These birds must now be kept apart from the others and as quiet as possible. Give them nothing but a plain diet of canary seed and rape. A little mixed seed should be offered once a week and a piece of hard, boiled carrot can be stuck between the wires of the cage and a little greenfood may be given.

The cocks will gradually become 'fresh' and should be placed in separate cages. At this point many breeders make the mistake of giving the hens eggfood and neglecting the cocks. As the cocks are in song, you may be under the impression that they do not require any conditioning; consequently infertile eggs are produced. I always try to bring my cocks into full breeding condition, as the finest way to induce a hen to go to nest is for her to listen to a cock singing.

Experience shows that, as a rule, a cock will be in breeding condition before his mate, but still the cocks should not be overfed with eggfood, and simply require a mixed diet. A good rule is to give them a teaspoonful of eggfood every second or third day. The hens should be offered about the same amount, but only twice a week. By this practice the cocks will be ready to pair up at the same time as the hens, or even a little earlier. A pinch of maw seed may be added to the eggfood, especially to that given to the cocks. A little niger seed will help the hens and a small amount may also be given to the cocks to bring them into full breeding condition.

The birds should have a bath at least twice a week and this is best given during the morning. I supply my hens with niger seed two or three times a week throughout the winter months and, in my opinion, this improves the birds' body condition.

Figure 4.1 Two types of bird bath and a hand held spray

A large number of breeders run one cock with two hens during the breeding season. I, too, find that this arrangement proves satisfactory, although I know that some breeders supply three hens to each cock. When I am going to run a cock with three or four hens, I select the hen which is the first to come into full breeding condition and run the cock with her for two minutes. If they do not mate immediately, I remove the cock to the stock cage leave him there for half an hour and then return him to the hen. If mating takes place when I run him back in this cage, I remove the cock and return him to his own stock cage. This will avoid any fighting.

GENETICS

Pedigree of a bird as we term it today is based purely on the belief that an individual has the genetic ability to pass on its 'quality' to the young which it breeds. Actual pedigree is only of value in so far as it can prove that no cross-breeding has taken place in the recent past.

It is an indication that an individual to which it applies must inevitably breed better young than that of a non-pedigree individual, but it is not completely reliable. Where any bird, dog or horse pedigree records are kept, only the individuals which closely approach their particular standard of excellence should be considered. Birds are close rung, which acts as identification of any individual, and proof of its pedigree. That being so, we should only concentrate on those birds which really do comply with their standard of excellence.

Choice of birds

If we pair together two close rung canaries from different studs, and if we breed just one which closely approaches the standard, we are satisfied. The fact that either parent has in its immediate ancestry a bird of some renown is not a guarantee of success. However, if both parents have come from the same source there is greater likelihood of success, since there is probably some relationship between the two parents, and a genetic link. The unwanted genes should have been eliminated and each will carry a similar genetic assembly, and when two such compatible groups meet we get young birds of high quality. Where birds are from different sources there is probably no relationship, the evident exhibition points having been developed by different methods of breeding. One bird might be relatively free from unwanted genetic faults while the other one will be carrying them.

I would never suggest that you buy the nest mate of a class winner unless it visually actually carried the points that you wished to introduce to your stock. I do not recommend anyone to outlay a large amount of money for even an average quality bird just because its brother, sister or parents had won prizes. Personally, I only bring into my stock (a) birds which actually excel in the required virtues and (b) ones where I personally know the breeder and have recently visited his birdroom.

The capacity of a bird to pass on certain outstanding features can often be overrated, and it is only if a pair of birds are genetically suited that they will then produce the required results. It is only after a bird you have brought in actually produces young which have the required features that you really know that it is a valuable stock bird; these are your irreplaceable birds. It is worth ten times as much as any untested bird, even though it has a good pedigree.

It does not necessarily follow that, because a bird has a pedigree and has won, it is the best, because winners in past generations may have carried all sorts of undesirable factors. It is always advisable to check the actual pedigree of the two previous generations then, if none of these record any of the features which you are trying to avoid, you can safely proceed with the pairing. It is more satisfying if the pedigree includes that of a near prominent winner.

A register which carries the details of the brothers and sisters of the pedigree holder would be invaluable, and you will be better able to assess the breeding capacity of the bird, and to know that it was a true representative of a particular nest, and not the only good one of half a dozen nests. There is only one way whereby you can truly judge the value of the bird, it must prove itself with its breeding capacity when paired to one or more birds. Let us look at how we may analyse our pedigree bird before we may release into our stock any undesirable characteristics which it might have in spite of its pedigree.

ANALYSIS

Firstly let us look at what we mean by analysis; this is a complete breakdown of a bird's genetic make-up. To quote a simple example, to see if the bird is a cinnamon carrier, because there are fanciers who will **not** have a canary that is a carrier. Personally, I would not object to bringing into my stock a cinnamon carrier **provided** that I was first aware of this fact.

Cinnamon inheritance is sex linked, so it will be useful if we understand how the sex of a bird is determined. Cocks and hens have pairs of chromosomes that are identical, but there are pairs of chromosomes that differ, these are sex chromosomes. It is in one of these that the gene that determines the colour of the bird is carried. Cinnamon came about through mutation, i.e. a spontaneous change. It is not a factor in itself, as a cinnamon is due to the absence of the black factor. Black and brown combined on a yellow ground give us a green bird.

Sex chromosomes

I have already commented on this subject, and how we have male and female germ cells, the fusion of which I will call a union. Genes are handed down from each parent, and it is these genes which influence size, shape, colour, and fertility. In addition to the chromosomes which carry these factors – and remember that it is a gene which controls the colour – there are also genes which determine the bird's sex.

Of these sex genes the hen is the determining factor as she carries two different sex chromosomes; in the male the sex chromosomes are similar to each other. The three chromosomes which look alike are known as **X** chromosomes, and of these the female carries one and the male two. Now in addition to the **X** chromosome the hen has an additional one which is called the **Y** chromosome. In the male the sex chromosomes are **XX** and in the female **XY.**

The cock bird has two **X** chromosomes, one inherited from his father and one from his mother **(XX).** The hen has one **X** chromosome from her father and one **Y** chromosome from her mother **(XY).** The cock, having two **X** chromosomes, produces germ cells (eggs) of one kind only **(X).** The hen possesses one **X** and one **Y** chromosome so she produces germ cells (eggs) of two different kinds.

On average, throughout her life, half of the hen's eggs will carry an **X** chromosome, and half a **Y** chromosome. The cock bird on mating will pair these with his **X** chromosomes and the outcome will be that all eggs bearing the hen's **Y** chromosome will be hens **(XY)** and those bearing her **X** chromosomes will be cocks **(XX)**. The sex of the offspring, it will be seen, is determined by the mother only.

The cinnamon gene is only carried on the **X** chromosome; the **Y** does not carry a cinnamon colour gene. A hen cannot pass cinnamon on to her daughters, only her sons. The daughter can only receive cinnamon from her father on his contributory **X** chromosome.

Summary

To sum up the sex-linked factor in simple terms, the hen can only pass cinnamon to her male offspring because she has only one **X** chromosome carrying the cinnamon gene. If she lays an egg containing an **X** chromosome the resulting chick must be a cock bird because the **X** chromosome of the hen will combine with an **X** chromosome from the father. This is not so with the cock bird. If he is a cinnamon, both of his chromosomes carry a cinnamon gene so he must fertilise all eggs with a cinnamon-carrying chromosome. This means he can pass cinnamon to both his sons and daughters.

If a hen is a cinnamon she must show it, even if she only has pink eyes, but this is not so with the cock which has two **X** chromosomes carrying green colour genes. If the normal colour gene (green) is present on one chromosome and cinnamon is carried on the other, he cannot show cinnamon because the normal colour gene is dominant over the cinnamon. Some fanciers hold a cock bird up to the light to check if the bird has pink eyes and state, with all sincerity, that because it has black eyes, it is not carrying cinnamon. This must be wrong because cinnamon-carrying cocks have black eyes.

To make this clear, some authorities state quite clearly that the colours black and brown in a canary are due to melanins and that these affect the eye colour. When both are present, a canary is dark-eyed; when only brown (cinnamon) is present, it is pink-eyed. All birds with pink eyes are birds which carry no black. It is hoped that the above will help to clear up all doubts about cinnamon inheritance.

Determination of sex

Now let us look at how these factors operate and, in so doing, determine whether the chick is a male or a female. Each breeding pair will produce germ cells which contain half the characteristic number of chromosomes; with regard to the actual sex determining chromosomes, the germ cells produced by the male will each have an **X** chromosome. The female will produce two kinds of germ cells, one which contains **X** and the other **Y**. It is a matter of pure chance which ovum is thus fertilised, and as far as the sex is concerned, it does not matter which sperm is fertilised. If the ovum of an **X** chromosome is fertilised the chick will be a male, as **X** meets **X**. However, if the ovum contains **Y**, then the chick will be female as we now have **XY**.

It is a matter of chance which ova will be fertilised, but on average the number of males and females will be about equal. In practice this normally is so, but in my own case each breeding season my birds consistently breed more cocks than hens.

APPLYING OUR THEORY

Let us now look at how our previous words can best be used. It is assumed that the normal aim when breeding canaries is to produce young ones of top exhibition standard in accordance with the particular variety's standard of excellence. The actual aim should be to try to produce a high proportion of show birds each breeding season. Since no stud of birds will produce 100% pure show birds, some of the less perfect visual birds will each be carrying desirable features in a recessive manner. Now while the actual breeder may himself not require to keep these particular birds, they can, by their genetic make-up, remove the visual defects through selective breeding, and be very useful out-crosses for other breeders, rather than birds of unknown breeding.

Improvement of overall quality

This part of the book is intended to act as a guideline for those fanciers wishing to improve the overall quality of their stock. To the beginner I would not recommend that he or she should go out and buy expensive quality stock as they would not have acquired the basic skills to get the best out of their birds. Before spending a lot of money on any canary it is very necessary that the fancier has fully developed two things: (a) the proper management of canaries and (b) that he has got it firmly embedded in his mind's eye just what the standard of excellence calls for in that particular variety of canary.

Inbreeding of stock alone does not effect improvement; selection of any stock which carries a high proportion of show potential should always be borne in mind, and you should reject any stock which falls below a certain standard; this is essential before considering any inbreeding, of any generation, in each season.

Line breeding

It is difficult for the Novice to select his breeding stock accurately, so I would suggest that he does not commence by close line or inbreeding. Not everyone agrees with the principle of line breeding, which basically consists of selecting what appears to be your most evenly matched pair of birds that you are preparing to breed from. From these two birds you select the one that is the nearest to your standard of excellence, and call this your **line** bird, and we will presume that it is the cock bird. At the end of that breeding season you select the best young hen from the pairing, and the following breeding season you pair it back to your line cock. After that breeding season, again select the best young hen which the pair have bred. The next breeding season pair this young hen back to your line cock. At the end of this breeding season you then

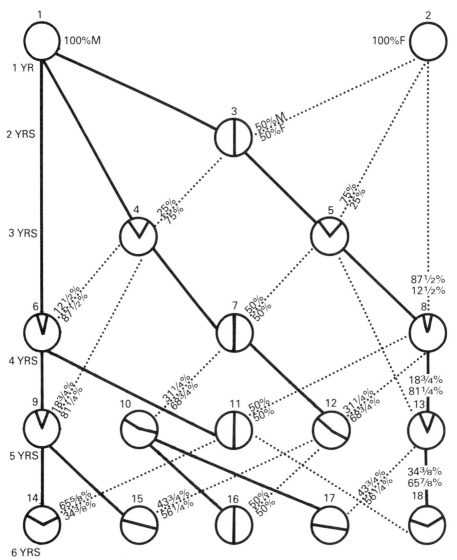

Figure 4.2 Line breeding chart

select the best young bird that has been bred, let us say that it is a hen, then take this young bird as your line bird, and the following breeding season pair it to a first or second cousin which excels in any weakness visible in line bird No. 2. This would give the Novice a gradual introduction to selecting which birds to breed from and, at the same time, practical experience of how to go about line breeding.

HOW COLOUR IS PRODUCED

Colour of plumage in a canary is produced by colouring matters or pigments that are carried to the feathers by the bloodstream. In the wild canary and the normal domesticated canary there are three colours, yellow, black and brown. Each is produced by a specific gene and transmitted as a separate hereditary unit.

Yellow

Yellow is produced by yellow lipochrome, which is of an oily, fatty nature and consequently tends to be spread more or less evenly through the plumage. In the canary, yellow is found only as a ground colour, that is the lighter colour on which, when present, the two dark colours of black and brown are superimposed in the form of variegation.

Buff

In a Buff the feather is thicker. The yellow colouring does not extend to the extreme edge of the feather. Its edging is white, hence the bird's powdery appearance. In a Yellow, the feather is thinner and pigmentation extends to the extreme edge of the feather. A Yellow is rich and deeper in colour than a Buff. One Yellow-factor can produce as rich and deep a Yellow as two Yellow-factors. Length or shortness of feather are not characters dependent on buffness or yellowness.

Whether a canary be a Yellow Brown or a White Brown, the variegation it carries is due to the two colours of black and brown together and of the brown alone. At present in the canary, no other colour appears in the form of variegation.

Melanin

The melanin carried by a canary affects its eye colour. When both black and brown melanins are present, a canary is dark-eyed. All birds carrying black have black eyes. When only brown melanin is present, a canary is pink-eyed. A Yellow-ground bird carrying both melanins is dark-eyed and its variegation, if any, will be Green, owing to the effect produced by the black and brown when superimposed upon a Yellow-ground. When a Yellow-ground bird carries brown, it is pink-eyed and its variegation will be Cinnamon, owing to the effect produced by the single brown pigment when superimposed upon a Yellow-ground.

White canaries

White Canaries are equal in type to the best Normals (Buffs and Yellows) in the various varieties. The breeder of Whites should pair White to Normal; from the former he obtains his colour and from the latter his improvement in type. The better the Normal bird, the better the breeder's prospects. Quicker results will be had by using a Normal cock rather than a Normal hen as the cock can be run with two White hens for, say, a couple of seasons, by which time the cock should have paid for itself.

Of the young obtained from the first season, the breeder should pick only the best of the Whites. It is from these birds, which should show some of the desirable qualities of their father, that he must obtain his second season's Whites. For this purpose a young White cock should be mated to a typical Normal hen, the object being to improve further the type of the resultant young.

The breeder may prefer to purchase a new Normal cock for these two young White hens, but if their father is in good condition this is not necessary. If it is a first-class bird, successful both at breeding and on the show bench, the wiser course would be to pair it to its daughters, which already carry the desirable factors inherited from their father.

This would, of course, be inbreeding, but the object of inbreeding is to obtain increased purity of one kind or another in one's stock. In this particular case, it is purity of type.

Recessive White

The Recessive White bird is homozygous (true breeding) for the Recessive White character. Mating two Recessive Whites must produce all Recessive White young. A bird bred from a Recessive White and a Normal Yellow makes a factor for Recessive Whites from one parent and the factor for Yellow from the other parent.

However, Yellow is dominant to Recessive White. The bird's plumage is not White but Yellow. By inter-breeding two such canaries to Yellow-factor birds, they would produce on average 25 per cent Normal Yellow young, 50 per cent Yellow-ground carrying Recessive White and 25 per cent Recessive White young. A single factor for Dominant White suffices to produce a Dominant White Canary. However, a canary that receives two factors for Dominant White, one from each parent, cannot live. It dies in the egg or soon after hatching out. Thus the Dominant White factor is lethal in the double dose.

DISSIMILAR FACTORS

One point of interest should be noted by the Novice; when a bird carries two dissimilar factors for alternate characters, such as a factor for Yellow and a factor for White, neither colour is affected by this association. Yellow bred from a Dominant White is as pure in colour as one bred from two Normal Yellow birds. And a Recessive White bred from two Yellow birds carrying the Recessive White factor is as pure in colour and as pure for the White character as one bred from two Recessive Whites.

Sample mating results
Some sample mating results are; dark-eyed White cock × dark-eyed Yellow hen gives White cocks, Yellow cocks, White hens and Yellow hens, all dark-eyed. Dark-eyed Yellow cock × dark-eyed Yellow hen results in White cocks, Yellow cocks, White hens and Yellow hens, all dark-eyed. Dark-eyed White cock × pink-eyed Yellow hen gives dark-eyed Yellow cocks carrying Cinnamon, dark-eyed White hens and dark-eyed Yellow hens. Dark-eyed Yellow cock × pink-eyed White hen results in dark-eyed White cocks carrying Cinnamon, dark-eyed White hens and dark-eyed Yellow hens.
Some pairings for Blues are; Blue cock × Green hen gives Blue cocks, Green cocks, Blue hens and Green hens. Blue cock X Cinnamon hen gives Blue cocks carrying Cinnamon, Green cocks carrying Cinnamon, Blue hens and Green hens. Cinnamon cock X Blue hen results in Blue cocks carrying Cinnamon, Green cocks carrying Cinnamon, Fawn hens and Cinnamon hens.
Some examples of pairing for Fawns are; Fawn cock × Cinnamon hen gives Fawn cocks, Cinnamon cocks, Fawn hens and Cinnamon hens. Cinnamon cock × Fawn hen results in Fawn cocks, Cinnamon cocks, Fawn hens and Cinnamon hens. Fawn cock × Green hen gives Blue cocks carrying Cinnamon, Green cocks carrying Cinnamon, Fawn hens and Cinnamon hens. Green cock carrying Cinnamon × Fawn hen results in Fawn cocks, Cinnamon cocks, Blue cocks carrying Cinnamon, Fawn hens, Cinnamon hens, Blue hens and Green hens.

ESTABLISHING A STRAIN

By now you should have all the basic knowledge of what is required to breed canaries so, finally, here a few words on how to establish a strain. The final aim of our hobby is the breeding and exhibiting of your birds, and you must not let disappointments in your early seasons be your excuse for giving up the hobby. I trust I have provided you with food for thought, because it really is essential to put the breeding of canaries on a scientific basis. You will find that, when you have learned what I have said in this chapter, you can then set about applying it to start your own strain.

Using a system
The time has arrived for this and I will try to outline a **system** whereby you can breed canaries of which a large proportion should approach the standard of excellence for the variety. The only essential thing which I cannot do is to provide the all essential 'fancier's eye' for your variety and your selecting of actual stock. This is very necessary, but this is something which the fancier will have to cultivate as quickly as he can, because it is something which **can** be developed if you really apply your mind to it but, like anything else, some fanciers will acquire it more quickly than others. It is surprising how much you can learn in one or two breeding seasons, and be able to recognise a good

bird from a bad one; once you are able to do this then you are on the road to success. Many fanciers who visit shows can readily tell the difference between the best canary in its section and one that is only third or fourth in its class, but it is the ability to recognise the show potential of a nest feather canary, or one three parts of the way through its first moult, that is the ultimate aim.

Fancier's eye

A 'fancier's eye' for a likely show bird can be cultivated by careful observation of one's stock, as well as a little tuition from an experienced fancier, many of whom will gladly go through their stock and evaluate the various birds for you. I receive many visitors to my birdroom, and with each of them I will run into show cages half a dozen birds, then ask the visitor to place the birds first to sixth and ask them their reasons for doing so. I then go through each bird pointing out both its good and bad points. It really is most interesting listening to the opinions of those new to the Fancy; I generally find myself evaluating **them,** and this helps me to draw their attention to points which they have overlooked. We **all** learn from each other by this process as no one fancier always makes the correct decision first time, all the time – never take exception to an opinion which is different to yours.

Improved standards

The canaries of today are bred to a much more rigid standard of excellence, and especially a finer feather quality. Fifty years ago there was not such a high standard of competition and this, in turn, has made all the successful fanciers very much aware of the importance of genetics and just how much the various genes control the standard of the birds we breed.

By now you might be asking 'when do I know that I have started a strain of my own?' The answer to that is the breeding season that you breed a bird which has a better standard of excellence than either of its parents have; **that** is your first positive active step to creating a strain of your own. I must, at this point, say that there is no magical way of showing you a ready-made formula for breeding exhibition canaries. However, once you have made a breakthrough by breeding that particular young bird, then follow what I have earlier told you about genetics; this plus a little bit of good luck in obtaining the right stock which does not carry a lot of recessive faults.

Observation

I, personally, do follow a set pattern insofar as it is based on the results of a pair of birds' young ones, by careful observation of the characteristics transmitted by the cock and hen to their young, and this will often show that the cock and the hen by no means play equal parts in passing on the vital show points which you hope the young will display. You will have to decide to what percentage the cock and hen have been successful in reproducing their outstanding points of excellence, and which parent has had the most positive effect on their young.

If you can correctly understand and are able to do this, then you should be able to select a pair of birds and predict correctly the chief features of their young, and you should be able to forecast from a particular pair of canaries the main features of their young. You must be able to say correctly what, in due course, the young cocks will produce in their young hens which will be outstanding in quality of, say, head and shoulders.

It is not my intention to tell you in actual words just how to do this as it would take away a lot of pleasure which you personally experience during your selection of breeding stock, and seeing the development of a day-old chick to a mature canary. Enough to say that the necessary ingredients for success are in the hands of the fancier in the form of your stock and exhibition points carried by your stock. The thing to do is to pair your stock so that they will produce young which readily display the necessary show features; it should be possible after a few breeding seasons for you to breed birds which are as alike as peas in a pod! To do this is our ultimate aim, and here are a few of the stepping stones which you will have to follow.

Test mating

With this in mind, you will have to evolve a system of upgrading your stock, or **test mating** your most useful birds, to find out just what negative recessive genes they carry; to be really successful **this is a must.** Without first doing this you are reducing breeding success to a matter of hit or miss, and it could actually lead you to the road away from success on the show bench.

Test mating involves, as I said, the use of stock which visibly carry essential show points to see if they are capable of passing them on to their young. This is essential and should not be passed over as just a waste of time in a canary's limited breeding life as I presume that, like me, you do not take the breeding season as a way of passing your time. Like anything else in life, if it is worth doing then it should be done properly.

To repeat myself to some extent, it is a loss of a canary's breeding season; this might appear to you to be taking a backward step but, from the result, it could be the means of breeding seasons two and three producing very good exhibition stock. Not many fanciers are prepared to do this, and it is why so few Novice exhibitors make their presence felt when they move up to Champion status.

CHAPTER 5

The Egg and its Development

All the animals and most of the plants of the world began life as an egg, so let us look at the marvel of the egg, how it is originated, its structure and, in doing this, trace the actual egg through its development.

FORMATION AND DEVELOPMENT

Let us see just how an egg is first formed and, to do this, we must start with the hen's ovary in which the yolk is first formed. The ovary of a fowl or canary hen during its laying season presents an appearance like a cluster of very minute grapes which vary in size and number. There are, in fact, two such organs in each hen, but one will remain undeveloped, the fertile one being generally on the left-hand side of the spine, to which it is attached by a membrane.

Sections

The basic structure of all eggs is the same. They differ only in the individual structure pattern inside them, and the various constituents. For practical purposes the egg consists of five principal parts; the shell, its membranes and air space, white, yolk, and germinal disc. If you break open a hen's egg in a cup the future young bird can be seen as a white spot on the top of the yolk.

When a hen mates with a cock bird they each produce a flat round shaped germ disc which becomes attached to the yolk. Each yolk with its attached two germ cells is formed, each yolk being contained within a thin and transparent ovisac, connected by a narrow stem with the ovary. The female cell, or disc, contains half the total number of chromosomes which are its genetic construction, and the male cell the other half. After these have become fused or fertilisation has occurred, these two cells grow and divide many times until, by the time that the actual egg is laid, they are visible as the germinal disc. As the yolk becomes fully matured the enclosing membrane becomes gradually thinner round its greatest diameter, which then exhibits a pale zone called the **stigma.**

Finally, the sac ruptures at the stigma, and the released yolk and germ, surrounded by a very thin and delicate membrane, enters the funnel-shaped opening of the oviduct, or egg passage, which conveys it to the vent, and on its passage along the ovary duct the white of the egg is collected, and also what will become the actual shell.

Ovaries

As I said previously, canaries have a pair of ovaries, but one of them does not develop and, generally speaking, it is the left hand one which develops. I have found that if a hen has a severe, prolonged illness from which it recovers, in nine cases out of ten the ovaries will have been adversely affected, so much so that in most cases it will not lay any more eggs but, if it does actually lay an egg, it will not be fertile. This misfortune will not in any way affect the canary's behaviour as a hen.

During the non-breeding period of a canary the ovary is reduced to a small shrunken organ, very small in size. When the bird is in breeding condition it enlarges and produces germinal cells, but although they are minute, they are rich in supplies of fat and protein and protected by a delicate sac in the form of the yolk. As the ovaries containing these yolks gradually grow so does the actual yolk. When they become mature in size the yolks are released from the ovary, one at a time, into the oviduct. From this it will be easily seen how two yolks may become detached and enter the oviduct at the same time, in which case they are likely to be developed in the shell at the same time as the white and shell, causing the double yolk egg which we all have encountered at some time.

Breeding conditon

A canary's ovary is stimulated to reproduce by the condition of the hen. This is a most important fact which all breeders are wise to remember, and our hens should always be given ample time to reach natural breeding condition; always remember that one swallow never makes a summer. During January I catch up all my hens and examine their bodies; when I blow their feathers apart, round the vent, below the skin, I like to see a thin layer of yellow fat. It is this body fat which is used by the hen's system to supply the fats for the forming of the yolk on the ovary.

Breeding condition is controlled by several different factors such as; an increase in the hours of daylight, an increase in the temperature of the breeding room, increasing the vitamin content by feeding such foods as fresh young dandelion, sprouted well rinsed soaked seed, and increasing the amount of hard-boiled egg in softfood. It is a hen's breeding condition that will control the stimulated growth of the ovaries, and then the all important egg development.

A combination of light, heat and vitamins is responsible for controlling the canary's brain and its sexual state. At the base of the brain is very small gland which controls the bird's breeding behaviour.

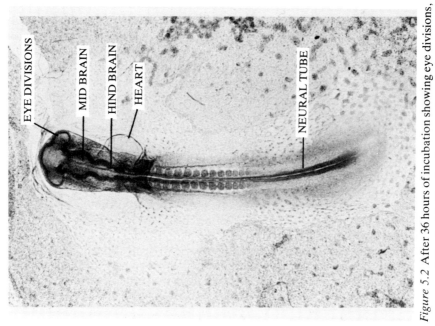

EYE DIVISIONS

MID BRAIN

HIND BRAIN

HEART

NEURAL TUBE

Figure 5.2 After 36 hours of incubation showing eye divisions, mid brain, hind brain, heart, and neural fold

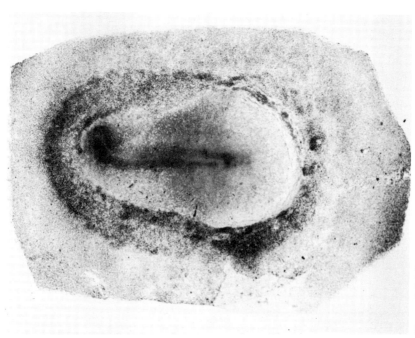

Figure 5.1 After 18 hours of incubation, showing the head fold

80

Anatomy

Birds have a single uterus, with the fallopian tube leading to the ovaries, which are near to the spine, and it is both the left-hand ovary and fallopian tube which are active. This is continuous with the uterus and forms the oviduct, which is in the form of a hollow tube which forms part of the oviduct; this hollow tube at one end embraces the ovary and forms part of the cloaca, or vent, at the other. Like the ovaries, when the hen is not in breeding condition this part of the reproductive organs shrinks into a thin pencil-like tube, very different to when it is active and allows the passage of the egg.

By the ovary the essential part of the egg, which consists of the germ and the yolk, is formed, each yolk being contained within a thin transparent ovisac, connected by a narrow stem with the ovary. These tiny eggs are of different sizes, according to their degree of development, and during the period of laying they are constantly coming to maturity in due succession until the clutch has been laid.

Development of the yolk

As the yolk becomes fully matured, the enclosing membrane, or ovisac, becomes gradually thinner, especially around its greatest diameter. Finally the sac ruptures at the stigma, and the released yolk and germ, surrounded by a very thin and delicate membrane, is received by the funnel-shaped opening of the oviduct, or egg passage, where it is conveyed along and, in doing so, is covered with various layers of albumin and other structures which are necessary for its development and preservation, including the thick white twisted strands that form the suspensory ligament of the yolk. Finally, a thin layer of outer albumin is added.

The membranes are added in the middle portion of the oviduct; this consists of two separate layers, upon the outer one of which the calcium carbonate of the shell is deposited. The chalky calcium carbonate is deposited in a loose granular structure on the inside, and this is used by the embryo to form its bones.

At a still farther point of the oviduct the egg becomes covered with the skin or parchment-like covering which is found inside the shell. In reality this skin consists of two layers, which can easily be separated and, at the large end of the egg, they do so entirely, forming the air-chamber. At first this chamber is small, but as an egg becomes stale it becomes larger, so that in poultry laid eggs that have been stored for some time, it fills at length a large portion of the space within the shell, the egg itself drying up in proportion. In eggs which are about to hatch it usually occupies about one-fifth (20%) of the space. It has been proved by experiments that the perforation of this air chamber, even by a needle point, is an effectual prevention of a successful hatching.

In the final stages through the oviduct the egg becomes coated with that calcareous deposit which forms the shell, after which it passes into the cloaca and is then ready for the hen to lay. When the yolk becomes detached from the ovary to when the complete egg is finally laid normally only takes twenty-

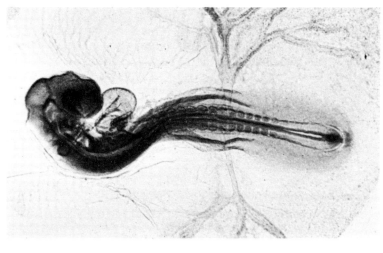

Figure 5.4 After 80 hours; ear vesicles forming, heart dividing up

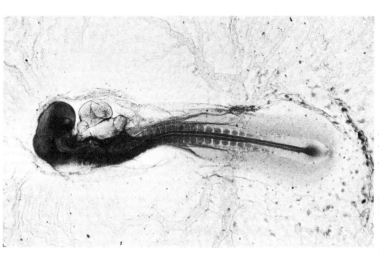

Figure 5.3 After 72 hours; body has turned to one side, head and eyes distinguished, heart large bulge, tail bud just forming and blood vessels clearly visible

four hours, and it is truly amazing just how quickly a canary's reproductive system works, and it could be truly said 'that it must be one of nature's miracles.

It really should not be necessary for me to say that you should never handle a hen that is in the process of laying a clutch of eggs unless there is a real emergency. Also, if the cock bird persistently attacks and chases the hen about the breeding cage during this period, he should be removed from the cage.

Egg shells

There is considerable species variation in the pigments added to the shell for camouflage. These things depend on some peculiar condition of the secreting organs, as does also the shape of the egg of each bird when it is finally laid. At the time of laying it is expelled from the uterus by violent muscular contractions, and passes with its narrow end downwards along the remainder of the oviduct to reach the final point, the vent.

There are occasional departures from the ordinary type of egg. If the latter portion of the oviduct is in an unhealthy condition, or if yolks are matured by the ovary faster than shells can be formed by that organ, 'soft' or unshelled eggs will be produced. If, on the contrary, the oviduct and its glands are active while the supply of yolks is temporarily exhausted, the diminutive eggs which consist of only white and shell, and which not infrequently terminate the laying season, may be expected to occur.

This, however, more particularly applies to poultry, though I know of some isolated instances of yolkless eggs being laid by canaries. Disease, extending to the middle portion of the passage, may result in eggs without even the membranous skin; and if the entire canal is in an unhealthy condition, yolks alone may probably be dropped without any addition whatever, even of white albumen. This particular occurrence, therefore, denotes a serious state of affairs, and could quite easily mean the loss of the hen. The canary should be put in the care of a veterinary surgeon.

THE EGG STRUCTURE

Let us now consider the egg itself, which is a more complicated organism than the average fancier thinks, irrespective of what birds he keeps or breeds. It is composed chiefly of prismatic particles, i.e. carbonate of lime, with a small quantity of phosphate of lime and animal mucus, so arranged as to allow for the shell being porous. For its thickness and texture its strength is quite remarkable.

As hatching proceeds, however, the carbonic acid and dioxide formed by the breathing of the chick, dissolved in fluid, gradually dissolve a portion of the material and thus the prismatic bodies are slowly softened and disintegrate. The shell thus becomes far softer and more brittle as hatching approaches, and so great is the difference, that if the edge of a fracture made across a fresh egg shell, and another across one hatched or hatching, be examined under a microscope, it will be instantly seen that the two are in a quite different molecular condition. Were it not for this wonderful provision of nature the chick could never break the shell.

Canary eggs are irregular in shape, with one end broader and flatter than the other end, so if an egg is rolled along a flat surface it will tend to roll in a circle. This being so, when a hen is sitting on a clutch of eggs, by placing her beak under them and gently lifting up her beak, the eggs turn part of a circle.

Pores

The entire thickness of the shell is perforated by many tiny holes or pores, there being more of these pores at the blunt end of the egg. The purpose of these pores is to allow the passage of respiratory gases, i.e. carbon dioxide and oxygen, and the control of the rate of evaporation of water. It is the opinion of some fanciers that a chick is able to break through the shell because it is weaker on the inside of the shell than the outside. This is **not** factually correct and can be very easily proved if you compare a shell from which a chick has hatched and that of a freshly laid egg.

With the shell being porous it is possible for germs to enter the inside of the egg, especially if the shell is wet or dirty, and if they penetrate in sufficient numbers, they could overcome the natural resistance of the egg and this would result in infertility. The porosity of a shell can vary quite remarkably from among the many forms of bird life, but here we are only talking about canaries.

Albumen

The outer and inner shell membranes separating the air chamber need no further explanation. Proceeding inwards into the egg we come next to the white, or albumen. This is composed of a denser and more fluid kind, arranged in layers which can be peeled off, in the case of a poultry egg, just like the layers of an onion. A layer of the more fluid kind is always next to the shell and another one next to the yolk, but enveloped by another dense layer.

If a poultry egg is broken in a basin you will see attached at opposite sides of the yolk two slightly opaque twisted cords of still more dense albumen, which are called the **chalazae.** They are not attached to the shell but to opposite sides of the dense layer of albumen which envelops the inner fluid layer and the yolk. They are so attached at opposite sides rather than below the centre; thus they act as balancing weights, keeping the side of the yolk which carries the germ always uppermost, and very nearly in a floating equilibrium. If the egg is turned over, therefore, the yolk itself does not turn with it but retains its position with the germ always on the upper side.

It can now be appreciated how elaborately and beautifully the yolk, bearing upon its upper surface the tender germ, is protected within the egg. Itself rather lighter at the upper part, it is further balanced by the chalazae, so as to float germ uppermost in the albumen. It is usually very slightly lighter

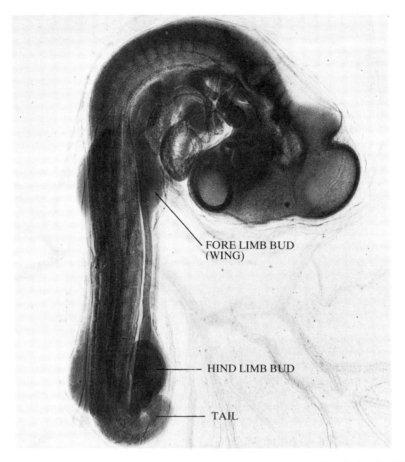

FORE LIMB BUD
(WING)

HIND LIMB BUD

TAIL

Figure 5.5 After 96 hours; formation of fore and hind limb buds with tail clearly visible

than the albumen, but only slightly so; thus it floats near the upper side of the shell at all times, but always separated from it by a layer of albumen of more or less even thickness, and oscillating gently away from the shell on the least movement. In a few cases it probably floats more strongly up against the shell, and these are generally the cases in which adherence takes place, or the yolk is ruptured during sitting time, but there is generally a very delicate floating balance. Nevertheless, it will be readily understood why it is inadvisable to leave an egg, and in particular a hatching egg, lying on the same side for any length of time.

Eggs which have been removed from the nest of a canary hen which is laying should be carefully turned over, through one hundred and eighty degrees, several times a day, until they have all been returned to the hen's nest. The shell being porous, and permitting of evaporation, such a course keeps the germ close to the portion of albumen which is very slowly drying up, and could be the cause of adhesion.

The yolk

Turning now to the yolk, this is contained within a very delicate vitelline membrane. It is composed of both white and yellow cells, and if a poultry egg is hard-boiled for ten minutes, shelled, and then cut in half, it will be seen that there is a flash-shaped nucleus or centre of white yolk, round which are several concentric layers of yellow yolk. Under a microscope additional thin layers of white yolk-cells can be distinguished among the yellow layers. On top of the yolk rests the **Blastoderm,** a minutely small disc. The difference between a fertilised and an unfertilised egg can only be found in this very small disc by the aid of a microscope. Using a microscope, it can be seen that in an unfertilised egg the tiny disc is whitish all over, except for small clear spots on its surface. In a fertilsed egg there is an outer ring of whitish material, while in the centre is a smaller clear circle, in which there are very small white spots. The chick will be created from the white centre spot.

At this point it should be made clear that from the time of the egg being fertilised and the yolk travelling down the oviduct, the future chick in its present tiny white cell has already commenced to grow. While it takes twenty-four hours to pass through the ovary duct, minute growth is taking place, and many divisions are commencing to form into a real living organism.

By the time the hen lays the egg, considerable change has commenced in the blastoderm. As the egg leaves the warmth of the hen's body, and it is not being closely incubated by the hen, it gradually decreases in temperature. Nature has allowed for this drop in the temperature of the egg, as the layers of albumen or white are very dense and are slow to react to either a rise or fall in the surface temperature of the egg.

Once the blastoderm reaches the colder temperature of the shell, nature suspends any further growth until the hen seriously commences to incubate her clutch of eggs; this is truly another wonderful achievement of nature and is not in any way due to the skill of the fancier. In other words, the progressive growth is suspended for several days until the inside of the yolk reaches a hatchable temperature once again. You will now be able to appreciate just how it is possible for a hen to desert her nest and stop sitting on the eggs and, if found while slightly above the temperature of a pot egg, these eggs (if quickly placed under a foster hen) will have more than an even chance of hatching out.

HATCHING FAILURES

Not all the eggs which our pairs of birds lay and sit will eventually develop into a live chick, and here are some of the possible reasons for this failure. Now, remembering this, as each egg that is laid is at the stage of an already live organism which has commenced to grow, it is at that stage also liable to

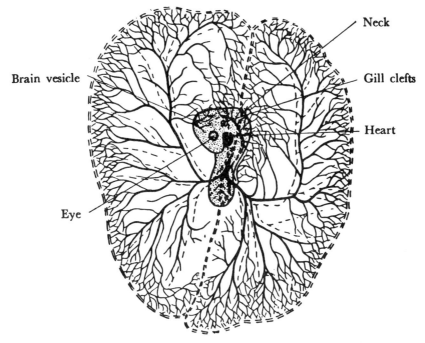

Neck

Brain vesicle

Gill clefts

Heart

Eye

Blood vessels of the yolk-sac of a five-day-old embryo

Figure 5.6 Five day old embryo

disease, generally inherited weakness, or any form of ailment or accident.

This being so, any egg which may be fertile, and where the germ commences to grow as I have described, could quite easily — and I am quite sure does — actually die through lack of strength. The question is why should this be so, bearing in mind that the hen has been in true breeding condition to be able to actually lay an egg. We hear the expression of 'a bird being in full breeding condition' be it cock or hen. It takes weeks for a canary to reach 'full breeding condition', and I feel that only too often we **think** that a pair of birds have reached full breeding condition when, in fact, one or even both of them require another week or ten days to reach that condition. In these cases the birds are not to blame, it is the fault of we fanciers. If you look in the nest of a bird out in the open after the young have left the nest, very seldom do you find any clear or unhatched eggs.

When I visited him at his home at Aston Carrant in 1952, the late Fred Bryant, the undisputed leader in the Gloster world in the 'fifties, was breeding young Glosters which had nests of three, four and five very healthy chicks, in large flights out in the open, each of which had six Corona hens and two or three Consort cocks. This was breeding canaries nature's way; we can all learn much by watching the birds in the wild at any time of the year. So it is understandable how we all at some time have dead embryos which are not strong enough to reach full maturity. Perhaps this is one of nature's ways of ensuring that only the strongest birds survive.

Simple rules
There are a few simple rules that Mother Nature has made and we ignore them at our peril. Here are one or two:
1. If, like me, you remove the first three eggs that each hen lays, make sure that your egg containing box or cabinet is kept in a cool place, because if they are left on a window ledge where the sun shines, as the temperature rises the embryo in the egg will recommence its growth. When the sun stops shining for a couple of hours, the growth of the embryo will also stop. Two days of this hot and cold temperature treatment will kill off the embryo before you even set the hen.

2. Make sure that the birds are really in breeding condition, **(a)** the hen to be carrying pieces of nesting material at the **back** of her beak and to **look** really fit and well and **(b)** the cock to be feeding his feet and cage fronts, and to be at **full** song and looking very slim and restless.
It is the all important word **fertility** that makes me stress the all important question of the fitness and condition of the hen as the prime objective. Serious minded canary fanciers must never let sentiment in any form be the deciding factor when it comes to which birds are going to be used for breeding purposes.

DEVELOPMENT OF THE CHICK

There is an hourly rate of growth of the embryo from the day that the hen commences to incubate a clutch of eggs, and if you look at a photograph of the inside of an egg which was taken after only eighteen hours of incubation, you can readily appreciate the growth rate taking place. You will be able to see the central germ spot which is now becoming oval in shape, and the outline of the head fold, and the spreading of blood vessels. After only a thirty-six hour incubation period it is possible to see the eye divisions, both the mid and hind brain sections, the early formation of the heart to one side of the embryo, and also the completion of the neutral fold down the whole length of the embryo. By the end of the third day the tiny but by now enlarging embryo, which is enclosed in the amnion, can also be seen, and round the surface of the yolk are quite distinct fine blood vessels. The eyes are now two dark spots, and it is also possible to see the pulse movement of the heart.

After some eighty hours of incubation the ear vesicles are forming, and the heart is dividing up into ventricles and auricles. At some ninety-six hours the formation of the fore and hind limb buds with tail are clearly visible. By the sixth day the allantois can be seen as a bag or sac protruding from the navel and independent of the yolk sac. At this stage can be seen the commence-

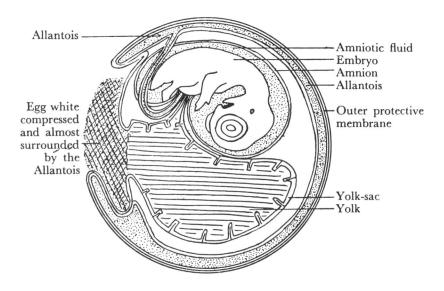

Figure 5.7 Embryo on the ninth day

ment of the growth of the wings and legs in the form of buds, which are visible from the surface of the body, which is also growing and taking shape. The blood vessels have now extended throughout the egg and, in doing so, have changed the colour or appearance of the egg to such an extent that most experienced fanciers can tell at a glance without any aid if the egg is fertile.

By the ninth day the allantois is now flat and spread out between the outer and inner layers of the amnion, from where it gradually extends until it surrounds the fast-growing chick between the outer shell and the membrane of the egg. From the illustration the state of growth inside the eggshell at this stage of its incubation can quite readily be seen, as can the development of the chick.

At this stage it is the allantois, with all its capillary blood vessels, which acts as a temporary lung by which the blood receives its oxygen from the air through the porous shell. The chick is not as yet able to use its own lungs until it is on the point of hatching. By this time the canary chick is beginning to show signs of its down feather-like covering, and its body movement can be detected; a lot about a chick's development is appreciated if an egg on its tenth day of incubation is very carefully opened.

On the thirteenth day of incubation the top of the chick's beak will have developed, or grown, a fine shell-cutting tooth which enables it to break through the membrane which separates it from the air sac, and the chick now for the first time breathes air. The chick's blood gradually ceases to flow into the allantois which has now completed its purpose and is no longer required.

Hatching

We have now come to the stage where the chick is about to break out of its shell, with its rapid body movement pressing the tooth on top of the beak through the shell. This is repeated many times until the tooth has cut away an escape aperture in the shell, and the chick is invigorated by breathing in fresh air which gives it added strength to break the shell in half. Hatching is now almost completed, the chick takes a short rest to recover its strength, and then works itself out of the remaining half of the shell.

The construction and strength of the shell is now very different to what it was when it was first laid. At the time just prior to hatching almost the whole of the remaining yolk had been absorbed by the chick. The chick's body now filled the complete length of the inside of the eggshell, with its head tucked into its body at the broad part of the shell, and it is from this position that any movement by the chick forces the cutting tooth, situated on the top of the beak, to break through the now very lightweight shell.

The chick develops a hard beak in the last few days, and its tiny movements inside the shell were helping to strengthen its neck muscles. It is this strength to raise and lower the beak over a twenty-four hour period before hatching that develops the strength of its neck muscles, enabling the beak tooth to break through the shell. Once the chick has hatched, these specially developed muscles disappear, as does the egg tooth which drops off.

During the time that the chick is hatching you can hear a faint cheep, which is the chick talking to its mother. From time to time the cheeping ceases as the chick, after its exertions, has a short sleep to recover its strength to enable it to continue breaking out of the shell. To do this it turns its head sideways, cracking and opening the shell, bit by bit, all this being a slow but steady process. The chick continues to stretch itself, using its legs and feet to press against the shell; it is these movements which finally part the shell, after it has been cut sufficiently by its beak; the chick can now fully stretch as it is out of the shell.

First appearances

The chick at this stage looks a little disappointing, as it flops in a moist condition, with all its fluffy down yet to dry out. An hour later, after another rest under the warmth of its mother, and we have a lovely little pink chick covered in silk-like down. The original wetness is due to the water in which the chick has been living until it hatched. The chick in turn shares this wetness with all other animals, because they all are protected by a fluid prior to birth. At this stage canary chicks are like babies in that they require feeding and cleaning by the parent birds. Now, a poultry chick is independent of these two requirements from birth, all it requires is protection from rain, and warmth.

The chick has enough of the yolk inside it to keep it in good health for twenty-four hours after hatching, but, even so, I always like to see a hen feeding a chick within two hours of it being hatched.

90

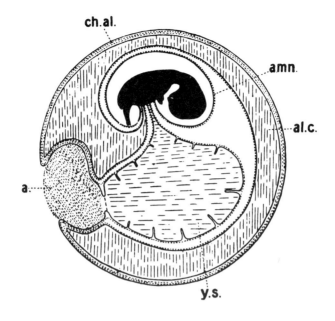

ch.al.

amn.

al.c.

a.

y.s.

amn., amnion ; y.s., yolk-sac ; ch.al., fused chorion and allantois ; a., remains
of albumen ; al.c., allantoic cavity.

Figure 5.8 On the tenth day of incubation

Fourteen days ago this chick was so small a spot on the yolk that the use of a microscope was required to clearly see it, and now it consists of thousands of cells which go to make up this very small miracle of nature. The chick has been created with all its genetic make-up, such as type, colour, sex and an instinctive brain of its own, and complete, automatic body consisting of a heart, muscles, air sacs, digestive and reproductive systems all complete in a minute form in one baby canary chick.

CANARIES AND ANTIBIOTICS

On the continent of Europe there are a very wide range of antibiotics which a fancier can acquire from a bird shop, or even from the seed department of his local canary society. I personally do not subscribe to this idea; researchers have found inside a canary's egg traces of antibiotics given to the hen weeks before, and even if they have been given with the very best of intentions but **without** a veterinary surgeon's instructions, more harm than good will be the result.

91

Now, on the other hand, millions of pounds have been invested in the production of chicken and turkey feeding pellets that not only contain all the required vitamins, but also various antibiotics in the right quantities to protect the young birds against disease. I have received letters recently from canary fanciers in the U.K., Eire, Australia and the U.S.A. who, during their last breeding season, have ground up chicken pellets and mixed them with their normal softfood on a fifty-fifty basis, and each report that they have bred strong, healthy chicks, which all had good quality of feather. No young bird showed any signs of ill-health or going light. The fact that during the winter months you have fed your birds on antibiotics could be the reason for a developing embryo actually dying.

It is important to remember that nothing can be added to an egg once it has been laid. Therefore, for the embryo to develop successfully, it must **already** have everything which it requires for development in the shell.

NUTRITION FOR STOCK

Any deficiency in a fancier's feeding methods is bound to be reflected in the breeding season. If only one or two chicks hatch out of five eggs, this should **not** be put down to a lack of condition in the birds until the feeding methods have been thoroughly checked. The bird's condition can only be equal to the fancier's management; if you do not feed a **fully balanced diet,** then the bird can never be in 100 per cent breeding condition. This is the reason that — especially after the show season — **all** my birds have ready access to a liberal supply of charcoal, for this contains a very wide range of trace elements. We must always remember that an egg must contain an adequate supply of water, protein, fat and traces of essential vitamins and minerals, and this can only be the result of a fully conditioned hen which has been fed on a fully balanced diet.

Condition

The word **condition** does not just refer to a bird's health, but all the conditions under which we keep our stock. Too many birds in a flight is **bad** management, even if you are feeding a balanced diet, because the dominant greedy birds will keep the others away from feeding, and this alone can create **stress** in your stock, and this is the last thing which you want to affect your stock. Not only will it stop your birds from reaching fitness and condition, but a prolonged spell of it will result in death. The thing to aim for is the feeding of the correct amounts of carbohydrates, fats, protein, vitamins, minerals, roughage and ready access to **clean fresh water.**

AGE AND ENVIRONMENT

Good or bad management plays a large part in both the condition and life of a canary; its development when young depends very largely on the

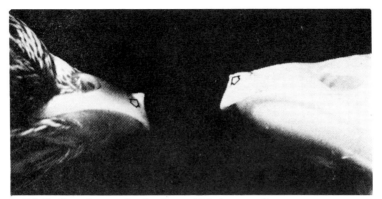

Figure 5.9 Shell cutting tooth of unborn chick (arrowed)

Figure 5.10 Drawing of a young chick two days before hatching

Figure 5.11 Drawing of a young bird showing feather growth

management at this very important stage of its life. Age naturally follows the next stage of its life cycle as does that of a human being, birds develop as they grow, until they reach their peak, from where there is a gradual decline over a period of years. The decline in actual physique, as a rule, does not occur until its reproductive ability has passed. The full physical development after the first six months is very quick, that is why some birds are in full breeding condition at ten months, while others take a little longer. The first two years of a canary's life cycle are its most vigorous, and the third and fourth years see a slow decline in its reproductive or breeding ability.

A canary is considered to be at its peak after it has completed its first full moult; this is particularly so in the case of self Green and Cinnamons, as their flight and tail feathers will then show their full **natural** colour. Normally an unflighted bird can look a little slimmer than an over-year bird, as both its flight and tail feathers are not fully grown. It is surprising how some canaries can, while they are five or six years old, still retain their show potential, especially if you regularly rub their legs and feet with a solution of **zinc** ointment and paraffin oil.

The actual development which is retarded by faulty feeding, can occur in

94

the first few days of its existence, or for as long as it takes to complete its nest feather moult, and this could be sufficient to prevent it from ever becoming an exhibition canary. There is today much less chance of this occurring as manufacturers have produced better softfoods, with more vitamins, than were available forty years ago, and the appreciation by fanciers of the high food and vitamin value of clean sprouted seed. Forty years ago we gave our feeding pairs plenty of **soaked** seed, before it had time to sprout and develop its full food value.

It was truly surprising how fanciers were able to continue breeding canaries during the war years when virtually all our basic seeds were unobtainable. I think it was only then that the food value of persicary, seeding dock, seeding grasses, plantain, chickweed, and so on, were really appreciated. The point that I am trying to make here is that the environment and feeding are both very important in the development of a young bird, but it does not affect the genetic make-up of our stock and its ability to hand down the desirable qualities.

This should encourage those fanciers who are systematic with their management, provided they practise the same approach to their selection of breeding stock. Where variation is due to the presence or absence of one or more genes, we then have the opportunity to select those of our stock which most resemble the ideal. The aim must always to obtain a high proportion of the young, which closely resemble the standard of whatever variety we are breeding. It must be stressed that the uniformity is very necessary in first-class breeding stock; the pair need not be identical, but they both must have a close resemblence to the rest of your stock and, of course, the standard of the variety.

CHAPTER 6

Management — From Nest to Show Bench

Of all things associated with the canary breeding season, the most important one is that of hygiene. Softfood and its containers, sprouted seed, water pots and greenfood must be scrupulously clean. Some fanciers use neither soaked nor sprouted seed, because in the past, when giving it to their feeding hens, they have had the unfortunate experience of young birds dying in the nest. They also obtained the same fatal result when feeding greenfood.

This is where good management comes in. If, for any reason, a fancier is uncertain as to the purity of the seed which he is about to soak, or other food for his stock, all that is required is to add a little **Vanodine V18** to the water in which he is either going to soak the seed or wash the greenfood. This treatment will deal with any bacteria that might be present in the food.

CORRECT CONDITIONS

During the breeding season I like to ensure that my birdroom has plenty of fresh air, at the same time being careful to avoid all draughts. Canaries really enjoy fresh air.

On balconies

In Spain and many other southern European and Mediterranean countries, fanciers and their families live in blocks of flats, and as a result have to breed their canaries on balconies. They rear their canaries in single-breeders, some with the plastic nest-pan containers positioned on the outside of the cages.

Environment

To breed canaries which will rear on average three youngsters in each nest means that you must have the right environment in your birdroom. When considering your canaries remember the old saying 'early to bed and early to rise' which is appropriate during the breeding season. The earlier in the morning that the hen will commence to feed the young, the more rapid progress they will make. Here is where the fancier himself can play a very important part in ensuring that his birdroom windows face east, in order that the birds can take full advantage of the rising sun and immediately start to feed their young. Moreover, facing this direction, the windows will not receive the full force of the midday sun.

I agree that an outdoor canary room should include some form of artificial heating, the ideal equipment for this purpose being either an electric tubular heater or a convector heater. Both should be controlled by a thermostat.

In full song

If the winter is mild, some of the cocks will be in full song by mid February, and many of the hens begin to 'slim up' as the cocks burst into song. Always remember, however, the old saying that 'one swallow does not make a summer'. It can be quite surprising just how long it can take the birds to reach full breeding condition. Fanciers should continue to give all their pairs adequate supplies of charcoal, which helps to improve the birds' digestion and fertility and also counteracts dead-in-shell which, in return, results in more strong, healthy chicks.

Charcoal also provides a good supply of nature's trace elements. I have been giving it to my stock for over 25 years, and during this long period the Borders have maintained a state of high condition. This breeding season I have been trying out the Australian method of including chicken starter crumbs mixed with my softfood. The only moisture to be added was that of a hard-boiled egg which had been passed through a very fine sieve before being added to the food and mixed thoroughly with the back of a fork. All the chicks in the nests have developed quickly, both in actual body structure and in feather growth. By the time they were a month old they had produced good silky feathering.

Starter crumbs

Chicken starter crumbs, used throughout the world, have been developed at the cost of millions of pounds. A mixture of these crumbs and hard-boiled egg has been used by several of the leading canary breeders in the state of Victoria, Australia, and, as a result, they have enjoyed the best breeding results for a decade.

I often consider just how little scientific knowhow has been devoted to canary breeding during the whole of the 400 years that these birds have been bred in the United Kingdom. But, on the other hand, it is amazing how the experts in this country have developed Type canaries during the last 200 years. Their feather quality and outstanding natural colour is superb. Take our Borders for example, which are not submitted to any form of artificial colour-feeding. We see some really outstanding Buffs, Yellows, Greens, Cinnamons, Whites, Blues and Fawns in breeders' birdrooms and on the

Figure 6.1 Adult variegated Yellow Border Hen

showbench. Why has the Border remained the most popular exhibition canary? Perhaps the following points provide the answers to this question:
1. It has a natural outline.
2. Its movement and grace are superb in a show cage.
3. The quality of its feather and the excellence of its natural colour are outstanding.
I am certain that in years to come the Border will still be holding pride of place as our number one canary.

Continued growth

When young birds have been removed from the breeding cage, it is up to you to ensure that their continued growth is maintained. Any interruptions in their growth rate, if only for three or four days, will be evident when the birds have completed their nest feather moult, especially to an observant fancier or a judge at a show. At a nest feather show, the quality of feather often means the difference between being first or second in a class where there are two birds of equally good type.

When your youngsters have been separated and are feeding themselves, and have just commenced their nest feather moult, at least three times a day you should cast a critical eye over them. At the first sign of a young canary being below par, remove it from the others to a separate cage which, together with the perches, has first been thoroughly washed with hot water and a disinfectant, such as Dettol. At this stage, it is a good idea to add a little Vanodine to the bird's drinking water. An important point is to ensure that the cage in which you have put the ailing bird is situated in a draught-free part of the birdroom. Chicks under the age of seven weeks which are ill will most likely reveal symptoms during the early evening, about two hours before going to roost.

Of course, the treatment to be administered depends on the actual symptoms. As a rule, it is advisable to remove all hard seed, such as canary or rape, and give the bird a small cube of bread soaked in a mixture of milk and glucose. Ensure that the mixture is not too moist and add it to a sprinkle of maw seed. Continue feeding the softfood, which must contain a high proportion of well-sieved hard-boiled egg. By all means continue feeding sprouted seed, which can be washed in a solution of water and Vanodine.

If an ailing bird shows no apparent improvement after 24 hours, remove the water and Vanodine solution, thoroughly wash out the drinker and re-fill it with a solution of water and Aureomycin, prescribed by a veterinary surgeon. I, personally, only give young birds antibiotics as a last resort. On the Continent breeding hens are given certain antibiotics in their drinking water before being paired up, and fanciers actually vaccinate their stock as a precaution against canary pox.

In 1978, while in Barcelona, a Spanish friend of mine told me that he had lost a third of his Borders. He contacted a veterinary surgeon, who eventually came to the conclusion that the reason for the deaths was that the birds had been supplied with too many different antibiotics. The Borders had become immune to this form of treatment when they were ill.

Special care for the moult

Pay particular attention to any birds that are moulting; the aim should be to ensure that all of them enjoy a quick, uninterrupted moult. If a particular young canary has a poor digestive system, no matter how good the vitamin content of its diet, it will not derive full advantage from the food. This will reflect in the quality and colour of the new feather growth.

I consider that the best young birds which moult out like this, but are of excellent type, should not be disposed of. Two months before their next moult is due to start they can be given a teaspoonful of charcoal each week. This should be continued until the moult has been completed. And after hand washing them, I feel sure that it will be found that the quality of feather will have improved. A point to remember is that a bird can only eat what it is given. At 16 weeks old, a young canary is still unable to digest its food properly.

Before and during the moult, I suggest you give each youngster a teaspoonful of softfood which includes hard-boiled egg, also a teaspoonful of sprouted seed. Also supply young, tender dandelion leaves, their seeding heads and roots which have been split lengthways so that the birds can enjoy the milky white sap.

Rape leaves

Tender, young, green rape leaves are very good for the birds, and they are also easy to grow. I give all my moulting Borders, both young and old, a daily supply of fresh, green seeding dock. This I consider to be essential if the birds are going to develop silk-like plumage with a lovely sheen. Those who are able to obtain plantain, shepherd's purse, chickweed and short succulent young seeding grasses, should ensure that all of these so-called weeds are supplied to moulting canaries. Referring once again to soaked seed, remember that, after soaking the seed for 24 hours, it should be put in a large sieve, and then rinsed for at least five minutes under a fast running cold water tap. This should be done during the evening so that the seed is left in the sieve overnight to drain off the surplus water. The following morning the moist seed is put into a plastic bag which is sealed.

With the aid of a fork, holes are punched in the top of the bag which is then placed in the airing cupboard for three days. When the seed is inspected, you will find that it has commenced to sprout and, on opening the bag, the seed will smell sweet and fresh. This condition is entirely due to the thorough rinsing the seed has undergone and the surplus water having been drained off. I would suggest that fanciers who have lost young birds as a result of feeding soaked or sprouted seed should first ask themselves whether they rinsed it sufficiently and, secondly, if they allowed air to enter the bag containing the sprouted seed.

Rearing

The best method of rearing young canaries which have been taken away from their parents, is to withold hard seed in the early stages. In fact, I would go as far as to state that I would withhold canary seed from young birds until such time as they have almost completed their moult. This system was adopted by me after having lost a number of nestlings. In my investigations, which involved experiments in feeding over several seasons, I reached the conclusion that, of all the causes of losses in young birds, the major factor is the feeding of hard seed during the first few weeks that they are on their own. I supply softfood with a little milk so that it is nice and firm but not soggy. I also give sprouted soaked seed which contains approximately 50 per cent of teazle. A receptacle containing rape seed is put on the front of the young birds' cages when they are five or six weeks old.

Fanciers have often sustained losses that they were unable to account for and it can be conclusively demonstrated that no canary chick up to ten days old can take a full meal of seed particles and live. A bird's digestive system is only partly developed at that age and can only cope with semi-digested food.

Figure 6.2 The start of today's Yorkshires

Many fanciers give their birds seed while they are rearing and, without appearing to create offence, it is difficult to teach an old hand new tricks. The majority of breeders have given little consideration to the fact that hard seed by itself is the worst possible food for tiny canaries, owing to the extreme slowness with which it breaks down and is digested. Young birds, newly hatched, should double their weight within the next 24 hours. They require a continuous supply of food which is very capable of rapid assimilation; no hard seed particles should be given which would lie undigested in the gizzard for a long time.

However, it is the subject of death caused by hard seed with which I am particularly concerned in this chapter and this is brought about in a purely

101

mechanical manner by the simple process of disrupting the digestive system of the bird.

The gizzard

A young canary's gizzard fulfils its functions as a part of the digestive system by means of a contracting movement. One tenth of an inch contraction takes place in gizzard walls of an adult canary, which keeps the food passing from the crop in a state of motion. The young chick's gizzard, unlike the hard muscular walls of the adult, is thin and delicate. This little organism, like a thin skin bag, has its power of contraction very easily stopped by an accumulation of hard seed particles.

While feeding by the parent birds is going on continuously, far from having any chance of contracting, it becomes hopelessly congested and distended with the food supplied by the parent bird. When this state of affairs is reached, the swollen gizzard can be felt as a hard lump and a young bird found to be in this condition is surely doomed to die.

Feeding

It is obvious that the breeder who has the opportunity of visiting his birdroom frequently has an advantage over the fancier who is compelled to leave the seed pots full early in the morning and is not able to replenish them until the evening. In most households, however, there is someone who can be trusted to attend to feeding the hens, by giving them a little fresh food every two or three hours. When the interest of the person tending the bird grows, no youngster will be allowed to die without a struggle to save it. But do not interfere with a feeding hen. Any interference can cause some hens to neglect their nests.

At this point I should like to give some advice to those Novices who have not had a successful first round. In the case of hens that are inclined to neglect and leave the young birds before they are old enough to feed themselves, the best thing to do is to try removing all the perches from the cage. More than likely the hen will settle comfortably on the side of the nest. With the parent bird close by, the youngsters will raise their heads to be fed and, provided that the hen is fit and well, nature will see that the youngsters are not neglected. One would expect that having sat so long and so patiently for 14 days and brought everything to such a successful conclusion, the hen would have her maternal instinct increased. But the care given to her young during the first few days of their lives is no guarantee that she will continue to fend for them. The experienced breeder can tell at a glance what the future prospects of a nest are. Full crops, plump breasts and abdomens indicate that all is well in the nest. If, on the other hand, the chicks appear to be under-fed and neglected, it is very necessary that he either resorts to artificial feeding, which can be a very tedious job, or gives the birds to a feeder hen or a pair of foster parents.

Hand Feeding

If you are going to hand feed see that your softfood and hard-boiled egg is mixed together thoroughly with a little milk so that it is like a paste. You can either use a matchstick sharpened so that you can scoop the softfood up out of the dish and into the bird's throat, or alternatively use a hand-feeder.

You will notice that it takes an effort for the chicks to stretch their necks and gape for any considerable time. Therefore, I suggest that with your left hand you gently support the youngsters that are gaping while your right hand is left free for feeding. It is important not to over-feed the youngsters.

I never like to interfere with chicks until they are 24 hours old as the babies are able to sustain themselves during this period. Afterwards, if necessary, the youngsters can be hand-fed at fairly frequent intervals. If a fancier is unable to look after his birds during the day then, of course, hand-feeding cannot be resorted to and foster-parents must be used instead.

WINTER-TIME MANAGEMENT

A friend of mine keeps racing pigeons and he aims for a diet not exceeding 22% protein. Canaries do not work anywhere near as hard as racing pigeons and should not need a bigger share of protein than that fed to racing pigeons. I prefer never to feed any ingredient in my eggfood that is not packed hermetically to keep it fresh. The direct result of feeding mouldy stale foods is listless, dull birds, easy prey to any disease that abounds in our birdrooms and aviaries. The risk of infection is there all the time, waiting for careless husbandry that lowers the resistance of the birds and makes them easy targets for destruction. You may say that you do not spend a lot of time cleaning up around your birdroom, yet you do not have any more trouble than those that are fastidious with cleanliness in their birdrooms. Well, perhaps the birds are immune to your bad management, natural selection or whatever. However, the test comes when you introduce bought birds into your flights.

If you breed soft feather birds like the Plainhead, Cinnamon and Crests, then you must learn to live with lumps and feather cysts. It is all very well to say we never double buff but, likely as not, the damage has been done long before last season. Some Reds and Glosters are now bred so soft that they, too, have this problem. Watch and handle your birds at this time of the year, and if a lumpy condition can be observed by feathers laying unnaturally on the bird, by running your hands over your birds you will soon feel the feather cyst. Check the keelbone at the same time and, if it is sharp, then this condition needs treatment too. These birds should be segregated for observation and possible treatment. The cause of the sharp keelbone could be a number of things; the least serious and most common is the fact that the bird is not strong enough to feed among a group of stronger birds. These birds should be housed and fed separately and sold to the bird dealer at the first opportunity. Since I have been interested in canaries, old-timers and successful breeders have told me to dispose of birds which cannot breed and

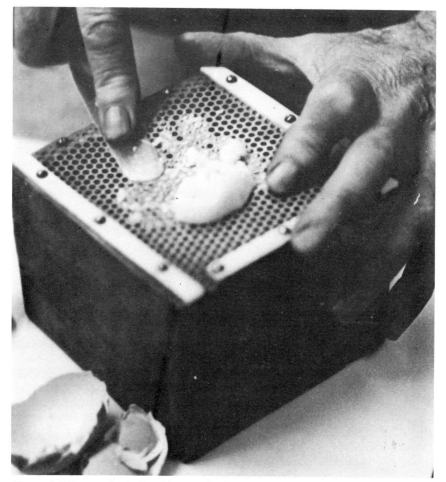

Figure 6.3 One method of making egg food

feed their young. This is hard to do, but it is the first sign that this particular line of breeding has degenerated and nature has no more interest in its future. What is more natural than a species of animal to reproduce its kind? We over-protect our birds and natural selection which takes place in nature is delayed by our mismanagement. Take a good look at your birds in the flight. It's a joke — how long could they survive out of your protection? We select our matings on looks or type and often overlook virility altogether. Be warned that if a hen does not feed neither will its young; it is hereditary and not caused by a nasty-minded bird. It is 'your' fault as she has had no control over her line and the make-up of the intricate genes that control her heredity.

CHAPTER 7

Preparing for Exhibition

Exhibiting canaries is, to me, like the F.A. Cup Final; it is the end of twelve months' work, both by you as a fancier and your birds and, unless the birds which you are going to exhibit are one hundred per cent in show condition — and for months they have been trained just how to behave whilst in a show cage — then it is a waste of time and money entering them for a show.

COLOUR FEEDING

For those new to the Fancy the following types of canaries have to be colour fed before they can be exhibited; Yorkshires, Norwich, New Colour and Lizards. This is done by feeding them a colouring agent such as Carophyll Red powder mixed with both their drinking water and softfood, starting to give it a month before the birds commence their moult and continuing it for a further four weeks after the moult is completed. The purpose of colour feeding canaries is to enhance their own natural colour. The difficult thing to achieve is depth of colour with an evenness throughout the bird.

This colour feeding is **not** permitted with the following varieties; Borders, Glosters, Fifes, Crests and Rollers. These varieties of canaries have to be bred for their 'natural' depth of colour and this can only be assisted by the feeding of natural greenfood and wild seeds, one of the most helpful of which is green seeding dock.

When a bird drinks or eats anything which contains **Carophyll Red** its digestive system passes it into the bloodstream which carries it to all parts of the body. That is why you must be very careful always to use the same quantity of colour-feed, otherwise your birds will moult out an uneven shade of colour. Some fanciers sprinkle it over soaked or sprouted seed with colour food powder and then feed it to their birds, while others will crush rape seed with a fine fork, sprinkle it with colour food powder, stir it together, and then feed it.

Figure 7.1 A Broken cap and a Clear cap Lizard of 1880 before colour feeding was introduced

ASSESSING THE CHANCES

To help you to assess if your birds are up to exhibition standard here are some of the things which a judge will be looking for, set out under the various breeds.

Borders

You should start by ensuring that the bird has a nice round head, and a bright, distinct eye in the centre of its head; the eye is also a guide to the bird's condition. The beak should be small and neat and in proportion to the size of its head, and the bird should be standing at sixty degrees on the perch. There should be a definite nip where the neck joins the body, and there should also be a nice rise over the shoulders and back. You should ensure that the wings are the correct length, just meeting together, and that they do not cross at the end of the flight. The tail feathers should be all the same length, and closely packed together, the chest nicely rounded and tapering away in a straight line through the vent to the end of the tail. A nice length of leg, which should be showing the feathers at the joint, the legs and feet to be free of any scales, all

Figure 7.2 A Border show cage

claws to be complete and gripping the perch. From the beak to the end of the
tail should not exceed 5½ inches (14 cm). The bird must be in show
condition with fine feathers of a silky appearance which excel in **natural**
colour, and the bird must have that delightful action on the perch which only
a true Border has.

Gloster Corona

This canary should have a natural roundhead, with the crest nice and leafy,
with the feather having a dark vein in the centre. The feather should leave the
eye visible, round, and excelling in its natural colour. The crest must have a
pin-head sized hole in the top of its head. The body should have a well-filled
back and its wings just touching and laying close to the body. The chest
should be nicely rounded but not over-prominent. The tail should be well
packed, and all feathers of equal length. The plumage should be close, firm,
and giving a clear appearance of good quality and natural colour. The
carriage should be alert, quick and lively. The legs should be of medium
length with no blemishes or defective feet and nails. The actual size of the
bird is diminutive, and it must be in good condition and spotlessly clean.

Figure 7.3 A Gloster show cage

Figure 7.4 A Norwich show cage

Gloster Consort

The same type as that of the Corona except that the **head** must be broad with plenty of feather over each eye; it must be round at all points with a good rise over the centre of the skull.

Norwich

This bird's colour **must** be bright, rich, pure, and level throughout. The head **should** be round, full and neat with the actual eye being visible. Most Norwich fail in the head due to heavy feathers coming over the side of the bird's eye. It should possess a short cobby **body,** with a well-filled-in wide back. The **neck** should be short and thick and the chest be deep, broad and

Figure 7.5 A Yorkshire show cage

full. The feather must be soft and silky with brilliance and compactness. The wings and tail to be short, compact, with good carriage. The overall size to be 6 to 6¼ inches (15.25-16 cm) in length and the complete bird to be well proportioned. The beak to be clear, short and stout, and the legs to be well set back and the feet and nails to be perfect.

The Yorkshire Canary

This is very much a bird of position which should be erect with a fearless carriage, the legs should be long without them being stilty, and slight lift behind. The feather must be close, short, and tight. The wings to be proportionately long and evenly carried down the centre of the bird's back, and to be firmly set on a compact and closely folded tail. The head must be full, round and cleanly defined. The back skull to be deep and carried back in line with the rise of the shoulders. The eye to be as near the centre of the head as possible and should have a good depth of colour which will indicate its good health. The bird's shoulders to be proportionately broad, rounded and carried well up to, and gradually merging into, the head. The chest to be full and deep, corresponding to the width and rise of the shoulders carried up fully to the base of the beak, which should be neat and fine. The body to be well rounded and gradually tapering into the tail. The complete size of the bird to be 6¾ inches (17 cm) with, of course, corresponding symmetrical proportions. The condition of the bird should indicate its good health, cleanliness and sound feathers with the colour pure and level. A judge will be looking for a well-packed tail which has a five degree lift.

The Lizard Canary

This is a unique bird due to its pattern of **Spangles, Rowings,** and **Clear Cap,** which are still the same as when the Huguenots brought them with them when they came to England from France over two hundred years ago. Lizard Canaries are now becoming more popular from what I saw on my last visits to Spain, Australia, and to a lesser extent in the U.S.A. Their numbers are on the increase, especially in Australia where, since my first visit in 1978, there has been a very marked improvement in their Spangles and Rowings. I would say that outside of the U.K. the best Lizards today are to be found in Australia.

Here are the main points to look for when selecting your show birds; the most important feature which the judge will be looking for are your bird's **Spangles** as these alone count for twenty-five points out of a total of one hundred points. These must be clear and distinct with no shade of light colour at the edge of the feather. All the spangles to be in neat, distinct rows, and to follow the shape of the bird's body.

The next important feature is the feather quality which accounts for fifteen points; this must be silky in appearance with all the feathers close together. The ground colour of both Golds and Silvers must have both depth and

Figure 7.6 Lizard and New Colour Canary show cage

evenness. The breast must show the full extent and regularity of the **Rowings.** Both the wings and the tail must be neat and show darkness of colour. The cap must be neat in appearance and have a nice shape, showing no sign of going down the back of the neck. The covert feathers to show their lacings. The eyelash must be regular and have clarity. The beak, legs, and feet must be as dark as possible. Finally, the bird should be relaxed, steady, and well staged.

New Colour Canaries

This type of canary is extremely popular in most European countries and in Australia. Just how this particular colour mutation came into being I have explained in Chapter 2. Briefly, they are in two groups, **Lipochrome colouring** and **Melanistic colouring.** The points which the judge will be looking for in **Lipochromes,** which are in two different sections, **Clears** and **Selfs,** are as follows.

111

Now with **Clears** you must remember that **half** the total number of points are given for **Lipochrome** colouring. Next, some thirty points are given for **type,** and here we must remember that the bird must not exceed five inches (12.7 cm) in overall size. Then there is the degree of frosting, and finally the quality of feather and the condition of the bird.

In the case of **Selfs** the first feature to consider is **type,** and then equally important is the **Lipochrome** and the **Melanistic** colouring. Finally, there is the degree of frosting, feather quality and the bird's condition.

Faults

In Chapter 2 I have given you the seven different shades of Lipochrome colouring and full details of Melanistic colouring. Here are a few of the faults which you should avoid breeding into your stock:

(*a*) Pencilling too coarse or faint and/or missing from the flanks.

(*b*) Light coloured legs, feet, and beak where dark colouring is called for. Alternatively, dark coloured horny areas where light coloration is called for.

(*c*) The light area local to the vent must be kept to a minimum with the obvious exception of dimorphics.

(*d*) No foul feathers or areas of variegation to be allowed in Self birds. A bird with any of these defects must **not** be exhibited.

(*e*) Where a bird is entered in a **Non Frosted Class** then it **must** be showing **no** frosting.

(*f*) **Feather quality and condition;** the plumage to be close and firm in texture, presenting a smooth, silky appearance giving a clear-cut contour to the body. The bird to be in full bloom of perfect health, clean, jaunty, bouncing and with a steady manner.

Type

Now a few words about type;

(*a*) **Body outline,** short and full to conform with the agreed outline. Back well filled in showing a slight rise transversely. Chest broad and full, giving a nice rounded front at an angle of 45 degrees to the perch.

(*b*) **Head,** a full forehead rising from a short neat beak, to be well rounded over and across the skull. Eyes to be distinct, clear, and bright.

(*c*) **Neck:** Short and distinct, flowing neatly from back skull onto shoulders and from a full throat into chest.

(*d*) **Wings:** Short and well braced, meeting nicely at the tips to rest lightly, yet closely, on the rump – tips of wing to end of rump. Flights to rest together, neatly tapering off gradually along wings.

(*e*) **Tail:** complete, short, and tightly packed, well filled in at root. To to be carried rigidly giving an all-in-line appearance to the body.

(*f*) **Legs and feet:** Legs well set back, free from scale, feet perfect, all nails showing.

Crest Canaries

Crest and Crest-bred Canaries are a famous old variety and are not very popular in the U.K. today, but out in Australia they are becoming quite popular with exhibitors. At one birdroom which I visited in Melbourne I counted over seventy of these birds.

Like the Gloster Canary, when pairing up during the breeding season you should only pair a Crest to a Crest-bred. To help and encourage fanciers to exhibit these canaries here is the *standard of perfection* to which they are judged.

The size and formation of the crest is the first consideration. A crest cannot be too large. This should consist of a broad, long feather with a vein down the centre. All the feathers must be evenly radiated from a small centre in the top of the head, the crest should cover the eyes, beak, and poll. The head should be well filled in at the back and there must be no splits in the crest, the ideal to be one which droops over the head and covers the eye and beak.

The body should be cobby and in proportion to its length with a broad back, with a gentle rise over the shoulders, and the chest well filled in. The tail to be short and narrow, the wings just to touch together at the root of the tail, and to lie closely to the body. The neck should be well filled in and the beak should be short and neat. The bird should stand up on the perch on short legs with the thighs well set back. The Crest-bred to have the same type of outline, wings, tail, and legs. The head itself must be round and large, and in proportion. With an abundance of feather covering the whole of the head and part of the eyes, leaving the beak visible.

Like the Gloster Consort, the feathers from the crown of the head when pushed forward should cover the end of the beak. The heavy overhanging feather which partly covers the eye is very necessary if it is to breed a good Crest.

Points to be avoided
The Crest must not show any horns, must not open at the poll or be split in any part of the crest. The head of a Crest-bred should be broad and round and not appear pinched over the beak.

Both Crest and Crest-bred must not have a long drawn-out body and this equally applies to the tail; the legs must not be long and the bird must not possess long loose feather on the body as this will spoil the shape.

Scotch Fancy

Although so few of these type of canaries are seen at today's shows, perhaps that is a good reason for us to take a look at them. This is another type of canary where **position** is most important, and here a judge would, in particular, look for a long, very slim, body, forming a distinct half-circle from the beak right through to the end of the tail. It has a distinct shape of head, being both small and narrow, which is only seen in this particular canary.

The neck to be long and thin, which should reach well forward when it stands at the correct angle. Now it is the bird's shoulders which form the highest point, and these to show no hollowness, and to sweep away to the end of the tail which should be well under the perch on which it is standing. This should give the bird the appearance of forming a circle.

The three main features for which some sixty-five points are awarded are as follows:

(a) **Style** or type, being well raised up forming a high circle. It must have a bold and free action, with life and movement.

(b) **Shoulders and back,** to be high, having narrow rounded shoulders, well filled in. The back to be long, narrow, nicely filled in, and must curve from shoulders to the tail.

(c) **Shape:** The body to be long, curved, and tapering in a half circle; it must be concave below with a nice clean outline. Finally, the feathering to be short and close.

Fife Fancy

This is the most recent addition to the Canary Fancy, it having been exhibited for some thirty years. It really is a scaled down version of the Border. Of its maximum one hundred points, **size** – not to exceed 4¼ inches (10.8 cm) – carries some 25 points; the **head** to be round and neat, beak fine and eye central to the head. **Body,** well filled and nicely rounded, running in almost a straight line from a gentle rise over the shoulders through to the tail. The chest nicely rounded, neither heavy or prominent. **Wings,** compact and to be carried close to the body, just meeting at the tips. **Legs,** of medium length showing little thigh. **Plumage,** close, firm, fine in quality. The **tail** to be closely packed and narrow. **Position,** semi-erect standing at an angle of 60% **Carriage,** to be gay and jaunty. **Colour** to be rich, soft and pure, as level in tint as possible throughout, no extreme in hardness or depth of colour, such as being colour fed.

Lancashire Coppy

I must say a few words about this famous breed which was extinct for some fifty years, but which now has been revived by the **Old Canary Varieties Association.** In its heyday it was quite easily the tallest canary on the show bench, being some 9 to 9½ inches (23-24 cm) in size. Today the **Standard of Excellence** by which it is judged is as follows:

The head, size and shape of the **Coppy** (Crest) receives 30 points. Second in order of importance is the length and substance of the bird, being worth some 25 points. The third most important aspect, which is awarded 15 points, is the upstanding position and type of the bird. Other important features are the fullness and thickness of the neck, the back to be round, full, and long. Finally, the condition and cleanliness of the bird.

PREPARATION

As I have said earlier in this chapter, it is a complete waste of time sending any canary to a show unless you have trained it how to behave whilst being handled in a show cage, and just how long this will take will entirely depend on two things, firstly a particular bird's reaction to being in a show cage, and secondly your own ability to teach it to display itself while being handled by a judge. Personally, I do not think that it is necessary for **any** canary judge to have to use a judging stick, provided that the exhibitor has correctly trained the exhibit.

Basic show cage training

I make a point of beginning the basic show cage training when a canary is five weeks old. At this age hang an old but clean show cage on the front of the stock cage, this cage to have a single thin perch about 1½ inches (3.8 cm) from its entrance. By the side of the perch place a little of the bird's favourite greenfood such as seeding chickweed or watercress.

Then sit in a chair and watch the young bird's reactions; this will help you to assess the nature of the young bird. Canaries are just like human beings in that there are those of them who quite naturally absorb any shock when, being startled, they will very quickly resume what they were doing. Birds with this kind of nature are relatively easy to train. Then we have the bird who is immediately distracted, disturbed and never really relaxes and shows its true self as long as it can see you. **No matter how good a bird is for type and feather, if it is of a nervous, highly strung nature, it will never make a first-class show bird.**

Once a young bird of five weeks old has become acquainted with the show cage, while it is inside slowly grip the show cage by the **base,** and gently remove it from the stock cage. Now stand still and let the young bird get its bearings. After ten minutes replace the show cage on the stock cage. In only a few days of doing this the young bird will have fully accepted this new routine.

Once the young birds are ten to twelve weeks old you cannot handle them too often. Now is the time to train them to accept strangers doing it. I suggest you invite a couple of fancier friends to visit your birdroom. After they have been there for ten minutes, quietly run one of the young birds in a show cage, slowly passing it to one of your friends and ask him to hold it and see what he thinks of it. The more that your young birds are quietly handled by different strangers then the more quiet and steady they will become. The birds should then be naturally relaxed when you send them to a show and they are handled by a judge. This is particularly true in the case of an open wire show cage such as the Border and Yorkshire cages.

Figure 7.7 A Roller song contest cage

Join a club

I should like to stress the importance of a fancier becoming a member of a local cage bird society, for not only do you meet your fellow fanciers, but this also affords an opportunity to visit their birdrooms and inspect their birds and methods of management. After you have been an exhibiting member of your local cage bird society for about two years this, in my opinion, is the time to try your hand at exhibiting at open shows. If, on the other hand, you wish to start exhibiting at open shows at the beginning of your 'career' in the Fancy, your initial outlay on stock will have to be considerably higher.

Hand-washing

It is important to be able to hand-wash a canary successfully. I suggest that your first attempt to hand-wash a bird should be made with an individual of little importance. The following is the procedure I follow one week before an event at which I intend to exhibit.

First, I fill three bowls with warm water in which to rinse all the soap from the bird's plumage. Into the third bowl I pour half a teaspoonful of vinegar to help dispel small quantities of soap which might still be found after the bird has been rinsed. Next I take a cupful of shampoo water and an old shaving brush or a piece of sponge.

With the bird held firmly in my left hand I dip the shaving brush in the shampoo and apply it to the dirtiest parts of the bird, namely the back of the neck and tail. I leave it to soak in for a time while I am washing the rest of the

Figure 7.8 Equipment for hand-washing canaries

bird, and finish by washing the neck and the tail again. I then rinse out the soap in the shaving brush under a running tap and apply the brush to the bird, always brushing in the direction of the feathers.

The bird is thoroughly rinsed in the three bowls of water. I actually submerge the bird held in my hand in the bowl of water, only leaving its nostrils and beak above the water.

I then remove it from the bowl of water and brush out all the soapy water from the feathers. This is repeated with the three bowls of water. The excess is subsequently wiped off the bird's back, flights, and head, and it is wrapped in a piece of warm linen which will absorb the moisture left in the feathers.

The chilled water in which the bird has been rinsed three times should not contain any soap. Only the smallest amount of soap left in the feathers after being rinsed will leave those particular feathers matted together when the bird is dry, and this will delay the bird's plumage being in perfect condition at the time of the show.

Hospital cage

Having been washed, the bird is placed in a hospital cage heated to 80° F (27° C) for about 10 minutes. At the end of this period remove the cloth.

In about an hour the bird should be completely dry and looking immaculate. The heating can then be switched off and the hospital cage allowed to cool down to room temperature slowly during the night and the bird can then be returned to its stock cage the next morning. For the next few days I give a light spray every morning.

Do not forget to ensure that your show cages are spotless with the spiral grooves in the perches showing distinctly. These grooves also assist the bird to grip the perch and stand correctly.

Those of you exhibiting Borders must pay careful attention to the placing of the cage label which must be at the opposite end of the cage to the drinker.

Show cages

Always make certain that all your show cages are spotlessly clean, the last job should be to give them a rub over with a soft, clean cloth so they look 'sent out to win'. This will not only set off your bird but it always attracts the attention of a keen-eyed judge, and ensures that your bird — providing that it is standing at the correct angle — will receive a fair deal. Win or lose, a well turned out show cage will always be noticed by your fellow fanciers; I have several times while at a show heard exhibitors say, "This chap always sends his birds out to win."

After a show I collect my empty show cages together and pour the seed into a large sieve. Then, using warm soapy water and a soft cloth, I immerse them in the water one at a time, wash thoroughly inside and outside, and then carefully dry it before returning it to a carrying case ready for the next show. After over thirty years of doing this I have found that, after repainting a show cage with a ¾ inch brush using Manders paint, my cages will last for at least four years.

For Border fanciers, always be sure to thoroughly sieve all your oat husks to remove any dust before putting them in your Dewar show cage, and ensure that the spirals of the perch are well cut. This will help the bird to grip the perch properly and stand at a correct 60 degrees. Speaking about perches, irrespective of the type of cage, always ensure that they are firmly secured and will not move as the bird travels the perch. You have to make sure that your birds are 'put down to win'.

POINTS TO REMEMBER

Test pairing

At the end of Chapter 4 I have written about test mating and perhaps now is the time to have another look at this subject. Perhaps, for example, you bring a new cock bird which has an excellent appearance into your birdroom. It will probably be an unflighted cock and, therefore, you cannot correctly say just what quality of young ones it will breed so, for the first breeding season, I personally would pair it to two different hens, both of which will have previously bred young ones which were of good type and feather.

By pairing the cock which has been brought in to these two particular hens I am test mating the cock, and all its young should be carefully moulted out, when you will be able to assess the cock's breeding potential. If more of the young do not favour the appearance of the new cock, then you can say that he has a recessive breeding potential and he should be disposed of. If, on the other hand, each of the two hens to which he was paired breed several young, all of which closely resemble the cock, then you have proved his breeding potential and that he possesses a **dominant** breeding factor. This cock will make an ideal **line breeding** bird and, after his second breeding season as a **line** cock paired to one or more of his previous year's daughters, he should produce canaries of a very good type of which some could even be of a better standard than the **line** cock.

The young birds that were bred when the cock was test mated and carried their father's characteristics would all make potentially good breeding stock, and should be retained.

If a Novice exhibitor uses this method of selecting his breeding pairs then, when he has to move up to the Champion classes, he will soon be breeding young birds which will hold their own when exhibited against other Champion bred birds.

Helpful hints

Do not use birds that have taken a long time to moult.
Do not use any bird that has an inherited fault.
Do not pair a bird with one fault to another with the opposite fault thinking they will balance each other – you will just have young birds with two faults instead of one.
Do not use any birds which are always under the weather.
Do not use birds with bad habits.
Do not use your best bird to anything else but another top bird – best to best always.
Do not use thin birds.
Do not use birds that are not in good condition.
Do not say that you have no mites in the birdroom just because you have never seen one.
Do not breed birds unless you are going to take care of them properly and are going to feed them well.
Do not waste your time and money buying poor stock.

Inbreeding is that system of breeding in which the closest types of mating are practised:

Sire to Daughter; Dam to Son; Brother to Sister.

Line breeding is where the matings are between individuals within one line of descent, excluding those which constitute inbreeding.

Outbreeding is that system of mating in which the individuals concerned are unrelated – that is so far as members of the same breed can be unrelated.

Ancestors

As each bird has two parents, and the same is true of its parents, and so on, working back through a number of generations the number of ancestors doubles with each generation, and very soon we come to numbers that are very much higher than the number of canaries living today. For this reason, it is practically impossible for two birds of the same breed to be entirely unrelated. At the formation of any new variety of canary, it is necessary to employ a certain amount of inbreeding until the desired type becomes fixed

— and thoroughbred racehorses were no exception. But very little, if any, inbreeding has been practised since the stud book was first published in 1808, although the pedigree of all present-day thoroughbreds can be traced back to three sires.

Canary fanciers could not do better than to follow the example of breeders of the thoroughbred racehorse, and breed only from the best or the progeny of the best. Dr A.L. Hauedoarn of Holland, in his work entitled *Animal Breeding,* recommends inbreeding — not to produce outstanding animals or birds, as some experts would have us believe — but to bring about a levelling up of quality.

The idea of starting inbreeding with canaries of mediocre quality should never be entertained. As long as the best canaries in a variety are not quite as we want them, crossing within the variety, or even cross-breeding of individuals of related varieties should not be resorted to.

There is no reason why two perfectly sound, healthy birds — no matter how closely related — should not breed young as good as themselves. It is not occasional inbreeding, but continuous inbreeding, that is to be avoided. Line breeding, if carried too far, will have the same adverse effects as inbreeding, and if we rely entirely on outbreeding, we will never know where we are.

Achieving a balance

A combination of line and outbreeding is the answer. Breeding is not an exact science and never will be — nature will see to that — but to make progress we must have a system to work on, and the best advice is to breed only from your best birds or their progeny. No matter how much you pay for your birds or how long their pedigree may be, you have got to create your own strain of birds.

When, du.ing the process of selection your birds become fixed in their own genetics, only cross-breeding would help in bringing back any desired feature necessary to improve some quality which has become fixed as a result of inbreeding — **inbreeding in almost any stock will produce a certain proportion of worthless offspring, which must be discarded.**

The object of any fancier is not so much to improve the average quality of his stock, but to produce the outstanding bird, and this can only be accomplished where there is consistency of breeding. Inbreeding means similarity, and similarity results in a strain of birds in which none is outstanding.

ACHIEVING 'IDEAL' BIRDS

For those prepared to think beyond their next First ticket and possible profit, this subject raises a lot of thought provoking points. When drawing up standards for birds, they must not only look attractive but be physically capable of survival without interference with health and temperament. We never want to deteriorate to the point reached by some dog breeds where they

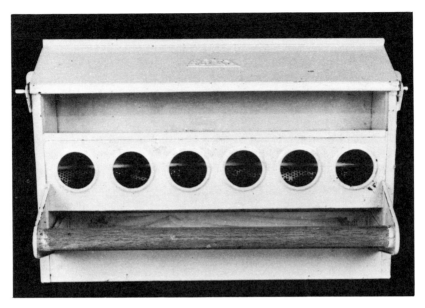

Figure 7.9 Aviary Seed Hopper

need vets to keep them alive and animal psychiatrists to make them controllable.

Sexual differences should also be maintained; hens that look like cocks may make good show birds but all too often are failures in the breeding pen; no matter what our ambitions are they cannot be achieved without good breeding hens. Care must be taken when altering birds' beaks; Mother Nature has designed the beak to suit each bird's method of feeding. There are already pigeons that cannot feed their young due to excessively small beaks and one U.K. Bengalese breeder said that, since they had reduced beak size for exhibition purposes, they found that they were not as good at feeding their young. Mother Nature only takes so much before she rebels, nature is designed for the survival of the fittest and cares nothing about the latest fashion.

Danger signs

The danger signs are there to see, any loss of fertility or vigour should not be ignored. Any breeds that need feeders are approaching the danger zone; in the breeding pen we must use only the fit and not use birds showing any tendency to deformity or weakness. The ability to fly is a feature of most birds, but one that is often temporarily lost if a bird does not get the opportunity to exercise its wings so, for the sake of your birds' health, give them plenty of opportunity to fly during the non-breeding season.

Modern investigation has shown that broad feathered birds need a higher protein input to promote feather growth than their finer feathered nest mates; it also appears that a bird's ability to absorb protein is limited and if more is absorbed by the feathers there is less left for other needs.

For years it has been well known that big birds are rarely as active or as fertile as smaller birds of the same family, but it is only recently that the feather-protein link has become accepted. While only a personal opinion, it appears to me that exercise increases a bird's ability to absorb protein and in turn increase vigour and fertility; of course they may only be fitter simply as a direct result of the exercise. If true it supports the suggestion that birds in flights should be fed a higher protein diet than birds in cabinets, particularly prior to and during the moult when new feather growth is taking place.

Figure 7.10 Washing equipment. Note jar of vinegar: a little removes any soap left in feathers while being mixed.

122

CHAPTER 8

Green, Cinnamon and White Canaries

During the last show season I was pleased to witness the increased numbers of canaries in the classes for Greens, Cinnamons, and Whites at the major shows I visited. I was also impressed by the improvement in type and colour. Breeders have specialised in Greens for at least 150 years, and it is pleasing to note the obvious improvement in both Yellow and Buff Green Borders. There have also been distinct improvements in the pencilling on both the body and thighs. Nowadays, you can notice distinct pencil marks standing out from the green background colour. However, the black is controlled in that it does not detract from the green background colour.

IDEAL COLOUR

Over the last show season, I saw some beautiful Greens, all of which were excellent in type, but all displayed a common failing in having a grey-black colour to their legs, feet and beak, as opposed to the ideal black. As a general rule, it will be found that a canary excelling in the black colour of its beak, legs and feet, will also excel in the colour of its pencilling.

When judging a class of Yellow or Buff Greens, if you have an individual which is outstanding in the colour of its legs and body pencilling markings, but showing a faint tinge of bronze colour in the tail and flight feathers, do not be over critical of this bird as it is almost certain to be unflighted. When it moults out, you will find that the feathers will have lost their bronze colour and will appear as black as the legs.

Extreme edges

However, if you look very closely, a very faint tinge of green will be found at the extreme edges of the flights and tail feathers. It is so faint in colour that it appears that you could scrape it off with a razor blade.

During the 1980 show season, while judging Borders in the U.K. and at the All-Border shows held in Victoria and South Australia, I was quite surprised that most of the best Greens were Buff Greens and not Yellow Greens which are of the type selected for specials by most judges.

Feather type

All Borders, be they Green, Cinnamon, or White, are of the feather type known as Buff or Yellow. This does not refer to the colour but to the texture of the feather. In my opinion, Greens and Cinnamons are the only two colours in which consideration can be given to pairing Yellow to Yellow or Buff to Buff.

If you have a Yellow Green cock or hen, which is of excellent type, colour, and feather, but sporting black pencilling which is too broad and tends to dominate the green background, it should be paired to another Green which has a thin pencilling. From this pairing you should produce 75 per cent Greens, which should make good show birds. On the other hand, if the pencilling of your Buff Greens is too thin and fine, you should pair them to Buffs which excel in pencilling and colour and, again, 75 per cent of the young should make good show birds.

If the background green colour of your birds is becoming dull and smoky, it is advisable to introduce a good, clean-coloured Variegated Yellow, which has been bred from black-eyed parents. This should improve the background green colour in the young. Care should be taken when using this particular out-cross, as it could lead to youngsters being produced with light streaks on the underparts, especially around the vent. These constitute a fault which must be avoided.

From an exhibition point of view a Green Border is not at its best until it is two or three years old. With regard to the actual shade of green, it is often said that the correct colour should be grass green. I feel that this description could be very misleading to the Novice. Having been born and brought up on a farm, I am aware that there are many different shades of 'grass green', according to the type of vegetation. Anyone who is uncertain as to the particular shade of green required should look at a young holly leaf; the upperside of which I would describe as that of a Yellow Green and the underside as a Buff Green.

Correct pencilling

With this background colour established in your stock, care should be taken to produce the correct pencilling. The markings should be dark and clearly defined in straight lines, but should not detract from the natural green background colour.

The term of 'Yellow Green' can be very misleading as there must be no signs of yellow in the green of the bird's plumage. However, Yellow Greens appear on the show bench which actually carry yellow in the make-up of their feather colour. When I was judging in Spain in 1977, 1978 and 1979 I found that the Green Borders did show yellow in their feather colour and, on enquiring I found that practically all these birds could be traced back to a pair of Green Borders which had been obtained from the U.K. in 1976. I feel that the main faults to be avoided in Greens are light streaks, bronze coloured wing butts and bronze thighs, broad, stubby pencilling and, finally, light-coloured legs, feet and beak.

Figure 8.1 A yellow and Buff Green Yorkshire, and a Yellow Green Norwich of 1890

Wrong shade

Individuals which contain Cinnamon blood should not be used by a Novice as they will carry the wrong shade of Green. However, for the more experienced fancier, there are times when it may be advantageous to use them occasionally.

In recent times there has been an increased number of Cinnamon birds

bred in most varieties of canaries. This grand old variety saw its most perfectly coloured birds exhibited some 30 years ago, but I have been delighted in
recent years to see a return of feather quality, colour and pencilling, similar to
those of the early 1950's. By this I mean that the large coarse feathered birds
have been replaced by ones of the feather quality of a normal, but at the same
time showing that lovely cinnamon colour which is the outstanding feature
of the breed.

My biggest complaint of them is the distinct pencilling on the back and
thighs. A distinct dark brown pencilling sets off the background cinnamon
feather colour. This should follow a similar type of pattern to that which I
have described for Greens.

Cinnamon inheritance in canaries

When Cinnamon inheritance is mentioned among canary breeders, varying
opinions on the subject are often expressed. How many times do we hear the
statements, that 'the trouble with Cinnamon is that you never know when it is
going to appear', or 'it's so complicated, I do not bother'. There can be no
justification for them. Cinnamon inheritance should cease to be a mystery.
Its existence has been known since the early 18th century, so it is about time
this 'bogey' was laid to rest.

While considering Cinnamon colour inheritance we should also
remember that Cinnamon has an effect on feather quality. If only for this
reason, it is important to understand its whereabouts in your stock, so that it
can be used to the best advantage. The general point of disagreement, and it is
believed the one that causes most controversy, is how the sex-link factor
works. A view strongly held by some prominent breeders is that if a cock bird
has been bred from a Normal hen, it has no Cinnamon in its make-up. Their
theory is that a cock bird cannot 'pass on' Cinnamon to its male offspring. It is
this opinion that conflicts with the findings of those conversant with the way
the mutation works.

Whites

Recently there has been a great increase in the number of fanciers exhibiting
White-ground Borders. In many respects, these birds have the same genetic
make-up as any other colour. Their colour is controlled by a single gene
factor and they appear in both Yellow and Buff feather types. However, there
is one particular difference, in that Whites can be either Dominant or
Recessive..

As previously stated, their colour is controlled by a single gene, so that
when pairing a White to a Normal, one member of the pair should be a
Yellow and the other a Buff. Most Whites available in the U.K. are Dominant
and there are very few Recessives. Therefore, it is quite acceptable to pair two
Whites together but, in doing so, you will not improve the White-ground
colour of the young. For this reason I always make a point of pairing a White-

ground individual to a Normal. If you are not sure if a particular White is a Yellow or a Buff, it should be paired to a Buff.

Last season I saw many Whites which were of excellent type, feather and colour, but their flight feathers all sported a distinct trace of yellow. One should not consider this to be a feature peculiar to Whites. I have seen examples which had pure white flights, with absolutely no trace of yellow in their flight feathers.

As I previously said, practically all today's Whites are of the Dominant variety which cannot be carried as a non-visual factor in Normals, whether or not they have been bred from Whites. **Any** bird not of a White ground colour is, therefore, entirely genetically free of the White ground factor. Neither its colour or any other inherited characteristic can be influenced by it.

I have heard a very experienced Border breeder say *never* pair a Normal to individuals that have been bred from Whites, because this will result in all the young Normals failing in colour. In my opinion, this is simply not true. Indeed, I would go to the opposite extreme and say that the use of a little White-ground blood will improve the colour of young Yellows and Buffs.

In producing my White-ground birds I try to avoid more than one generation of double buffing, so as to maintain feather pattern and quality. In doing this, it should be quite possible to maintain colour in the Yellow-ground birds and, at the same time, to produce Whites excelling in colour.

Blues and Fawns

In order to produce Blues and Fawns, pair a White-ground to a Self Green or a Self Cinnamon. Some of the resultant youngsters will be Blues and Fawns, either Selfs or Variegateds. This is because White-ground genes will mask those of the Green, thus producing Blue, and will mask the Cinnamon, thus making Fawn. Remember that young birds must clearly carry the Blue and Fawn colour. In order to do this, you must ensure that the parents really do excel in their own natural colour.

You can breed a good Blue from a Green which, in reality, carries little or no actual green in its feathers. From this pairing you will, in turn, not breed true coloured Blues, but only dark-coloured birds. The same remarks are applicable to Cinnamons producing Fawns, but the black markings will be replaced by brown ones.

Not experienced

Fanciers who are not really experienced in breeding Clear White-ground Borders must first learn to distinguish between a Yellow White and a Buff White. If you already have a Clear White-ground specimen in your possession and are uncertain as to its colour, I would suggest that you play safe and pair this individual to a Clear Buff.

CHAPTER 9

Type Canaries

The British **type** canary has now been taken up by breeders in Belgium, Holland, Denmark, West Germany, Spain, America, Canada, South Africa, Australia, New Zealand and most European countries. Practically all these countries have accepted the British **Standard of Excellence** with only minor alterations. On the continent of Europe there are two very distinct departures from the way that canaries are staged and judged in the U.K.

EUROPEAN SHOWS

In Europe a society which actually stages a show is responsible for providing the individual show cage, complete with seed, water container and floor covering. Every show cage has to be identical in both its construction and the colour in which it has been painted. Some of the larger canary societies will own, store and prepare for show use between two and four thousand cages. This can represent a considerable amount of both capital expenditure and storage space. It also involves more work for show stewards and officials than we are used to.

At many of these shows I found that the main sections of the staging are constructed of heavy gauge angle iron and are very rigid and safe. Their standard type show cage then just slots in between lengths of angle iron. All the staging is normally painted black, which has an enamel gloss finish, and looks very attractive.

Arrangement

The show cages are generally arranged four rows deep; underneath the bottom row at the larger shows there are garlands festooned along of fresh bright green laurel leaves. Dotted about will be tubs containing miniature shrubs and Aspidistra plants, and so on. Some shows that I have visited cover the whole of the show hall floor with matting, which is vacuumed over each morning before the public is allowed in. The actual shows varied in length of time between two and seven days, so this often means that there will be two or more stewards looking after the well-being of the exhibits in every section.

Show cages

Having but a single standard type of show cage, which resembles a U.K. budgerigar show cage, even in colour, means that all the different **type** canaries are exhibited in the same type of cage. I must say that when I first saw birds staged in this way, to me both the Borders and the Yorkshires lacked their customary appearance, individuality and appeal. To me it made the European shows appear very regimented, and lacking the customary individuality of the personality of the various breeds of canary. Unlike many U.K. shows, no European fancier would ever attempt to lift a show cage off the actual staging so as to have a close look at an exhibit.

Exhibitors take their birds to a show in a large portable carrying case, which could have a dozen small compartments, each complete with a door just large enough to enable the exhibitor to put in his hand to catch up the bird inside.

Arrival at the show

On arriving at the show hall the exhibitor will find a table, and two officials sitting down. The first official has no entry form or paperwork of any kind; the second official has the show entry form and also a ring number register. Behind these two officials are stacked large numbers of show cages ready to receive the canary and its class label, and also six or seven stewards.

The exhibitor places his compact carrying case on the official table and gives his name. The secretary then finds his entry form and asks for his ring number. The exhibitor gives his number and this is checked in the register. Then, one at a time, he opens a door of his carrying case and catches up the bird inside and hands it to the first official, who examines the bird's ring and calls out its number. If this complies with the ring number register for that exhibitor the secretary calls out its class number and the exhibitor will then place that class label on an empty cage and hand it to the first official, who then places the bird in the show cage and hands it to a steward who places it in its class on the staging.

Lifting the birds

At the longer, larger shows, the exhibition lifting card is stamped with the time that he can lift his birds, which could be anything between 10 a.m. and 5 p.m., and if he goes before he is due, he goes back to the end of the list.

When you lift your birds you hand your lifting card to a steward, then together you take the show cages to the checking-out table where there are two officials, as before. You hand your lifting card to the first official, who catches up the bird, examines its ring and calls out its number to the second official who again checks it with the ring register to ensure that it is your bird. Needless to say, you can only exhibit birds which you have actually bred yourself. To me this is something which British Border breeders would do well to copy. The lead for this should come from the Border Convention

Figure 9.1 Table show at a club meeting night at the Barcelona Canary Club

meeting held each April; it would quickly stop the habit of some fanciers bringing in birds and then selling them as their line bred stock.

CONTINENTAL JUDGING PROCEDURE

When I was first invited to judge type canaries in Europe it was at the December 1978 Barcelona Canary Union Show, which lasted for seven days, comprising of one day receiving birds, two days for judging the birds, three days for exhibitors and fanciers to visit the Show, and one day for exhibitors to lift their birds.

I arrived at the Show Hall at 8.45 a.m., as judging was due to start at 9 a.m. prompt. I was introduced to my Spanish interpreter, who took me along to where I had to judge all the type canaries. Here, I found no judging stand, only a small card-size table and a chair. There was a judging slip for each individual bird in every class, and printed on the judging slip for each individual variety or type of canary was its actual standard of excellence, with the number of points left blank.

I soon found that the judge sat at this small table and, if I was judging a class of some thirty canaries, the steward put on my judging table a single show cage and then stood back. I had to look at it and asses its standard of excellence in actual points, and then record them on that particular bird's judging slip. This was repeated thirty times until the whole class had been judged! The judging slips were then handed to the Show Secretary, who

Figure 9.2 Barcelona Canary Club show

checked through them, placing them in order of the number of points the bird had been given. The only time I saw more than one bird at a time was if two or more birds in one section had equal points; I then had to select a best bird in its section. Otherwise all Special Awards were made by the Show Secretary from the actual judging slips. No wonder two whole days were allocated for judging.

Barcelona Canary Union Show 1979

When I was again invited to judge the Barcelona Canary Union Show in 1979, before sitting down at the judging table, I decided to have a look at the **Posture** or **Type Canaries** first, while they were on the show staging in class order, so that I had a good idea of the overall standard of bird I had to judge. While I was looking at the Gloster Consort birds, my first impression was of a large variation of type, so I walked round the class a second time, when I suddenly realised that some of the birds were **not** Gloster Consorts.

Disqualification
I picked out twelve cages and said to my interpreter; "These twelve cages are disqualified!" He looked very surprised and said, "We do not disqualify canaries in Spain, what have I to do?" I then explained to him that all twelve birds were cross-bred between a Consort and a New Colour Canary, but that they had not been colour fed. Eleven of the cages had a blue disc on, which indicated that the bird was for sale.

131

Shortly after the show had opened, one exhibitor went to the Show Secretary and complained that "the English judge had disqualified eleven of his birds which were all for sale – why had he done it? No-one would want to buy them!" When I was told about this, I felt quite pleased and said, "Good – that will teach him not to try it again!" Nevertheless, the show was really enjoyable and I met many really interested fanciers who bred **Posture Canaries.** The Lizard Canary is quite popular in North-East Spain, and had quite good Spangles and Rowings, but their clear capped birds were often found to be over-capped.

South Africa

The most popular canary exhibited in South Africa is the Gloster Canary. When I judged at the 1979 National Exhibition held at Alexandra Palace, I met a keen Gloster breeder who lived in Durban, South Africa. We both watched the judging for the Best Canary and then we visited the Gloster section.

From his remarks, the South African Gloster, while being a nice diminutive bird, had not got the head qualities of a U.K. Corona; he really admired the class winners which we looked at. Their Consorts, I understand, did not possess that thick well-controlled feather over the eye, so I explained to him that this was the main reason why they were not breeding Coronas of a really high standard.

Australia

The best Consorts which I have seen outside the U.K. were in the State of Victoria, Australia. They had been bred by a young chap who was still at High School – Michael Andrews; for the last two years – 1980 and 1981 – he has exhibited the Best Consort at the Australian Inter-State Shows.

Australia really is the place for a canary fancier to visit, especially if you can be there for the months of May, June and July, when they hold their shows. Out there they have accepted the U.K. standard of excellence for every type of canary. They are very knowledgeable fanciers, many of whom are ladies, who hold a variety of official positions at their local clubs. Two very prominent Specialist Clubs, the Border Fancy Clubs of both South Australia and Queensland, each have a long serving lady secretary, both of whom are held in high esteem outside their own States.

Europe

While the U.K. has led the world in the development of the **type** Canary, it is the continent of Europe which has done most to develop the **Roller** and **New Colour** Canaries. The first fancier in the world to breed a white ground canary came from Europe also.

Figure 9.3 The Australian Plainhead Canary; 1982 Standard of Excellence

Standard of excellence

	Points
Head – Full, broad, round skull, and small beak	15
Neck – Strong, moderate length, and curved at the back	15
Type — Short and cobby, length 6½ inches, carriage stylish	25
Back – To be clean to the end of the wings	5
Wings and Tail – Short and compact	10
Feather – Short, soft and silky	10
Colour – Rich, pure and even throughout	10
Legs and Feet – Clean and free from scales	5
Staging – Cleanliness of bird and cage	5
	Total 100

Owing to import and export regulations, this canary is only to be found in the different States of Australia.

Australian Plainhead Canary

I was surprised at the excellent feather quality of Australian canaries generally, and in particular the 'Australian Plainhead Canary'. For a 6½ inch (16.5 cm) bird its feathers looked as good as a Gloster Canary. This is an unusual shaped canary which has a large, round head similar to a Norwich, with a perfectly visible eye in the centre of its head, a rather thick, long neck, almost vertical, with a back sloping away at 45⁰ and terminating in a short, well packed tail. It stands on an upright pair of legs and stands well off the perch.

Figure 9.4 Young Canaries (3 days old)

CHAPTER 10

Winter-Time Management

SEASON OF PREPARATION

The winter is regarded by some fanciers as a waiting period between the end of the show season and the commencement of the breeding season, at the end of March. It should be a very important time of the year, spent preparing your birds for the coming breeding season.

The months of January and February often decide whether you will have a good or an indifferent breeding season and, during this period, time should be spent in the birdroom paying particular attention to the hens. It is very important that they are correctly conditioned; a bath is hung on the front of their cage every other day; softfood is fed three times a week; and twice a week Parrish's chemical food is put in their drinking water.

The hens are normally kept five to each treble breeder and the cocks placed in single breeding cages. Last year, I kept fourteen hens and six cocks to breed from; two of the latter were paired up to four different hens in the first round.

Balanced diet

At this time of year try to give the birds a fully balanced diet. Besides softfood, they should have condition seed twice a week and some form of greenfood every day, such as watercress or the outer leaves of sprouts. Make a point of giving the hens a little bread and milk twice a week. Not only is this good for them, but it is invaluable in the breeding season and the young will thrive on it. So this will pay golden dividends in April, May, June and July.

Essential needs

In January handle each bird and blow the feathers on the chest apart and examine their bodies for any sign of ill health. All toenails are cut, and the feathers growing near to the vent are trimmed back but care is taken not to cut any of the vent guide feathers.

135

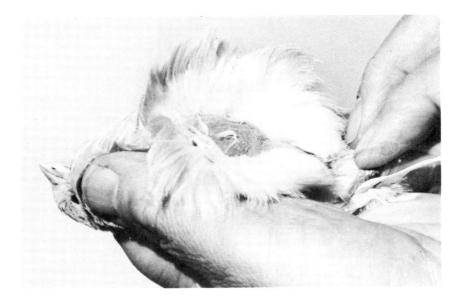

Figure 10.1 The correct way to hold a canary to examine its baby

How to hold a canary

There is an art in catching and holding the bird when any examination is required; there should be no hurry or fluster but movement of the hand should be positive. Do not grip too tightly; it is better to let the bird go and to have another try.

To examine either the back or the breast, lay the bird on the palm of the hand; with the thumb across the neck it cannot escape and if the thumb and forefinger are touching, but allowing just sufficient space for the bird's neck, so that it cannot slip through, the body can be given perfect freedom, the palm of the hand bearing its weight.

Ensure that all the hens have a plentiful supply of cuttlefish bone. I stopped using grit fifteen years ago and fed charcoal instead. Since then I have not had a single thin-shelled egg or a hen that has become egg-bound.

Recording results

I have recorded the results of the last three breeding seasons and it shows that from every clutch of eggs laid, I ended up with three young birds actually on the sticks. I believe the most important factor is the fitness of the birds at the time they are paired up.

After I have selected my breeding pairs, during the latter part of January, the pairs are held together in breeding cages and left together for at least a fortnight. Each hen gets to know the cock bird and normally no difficulties are experienced when the time comes to pair them up to breed.

NESTING PREPARATION

I use the earthenware type of nest-pan with a rounded lining sewn inside. The nest-pan rests on a ring made from Twilweld wire so that it is about 1 inch (2.5 cm) from the floor. There are several reasons for this:

1. Nest-pan is easy to lift in and out if this becomes necessary.
2. It is in a position where it is readily accessible to handle the eggs when the hen lays.
3. If a young bird is actually dragged out of the nest by the hen it cannot fall far and then only on the wood shavings.
4. When the young are 16—17 days old, if they stand on the edge of the nest and hop on to the floor of the cage, they can quite easily get back to the nest themselves.

For nest-building material old carpet underfelt of the non-fibrous kind is recommended, which does not get under the small scales of the birds' legs and feet, causing them an injury. It should be washed before use.

FOOD HINTS

Canaries like carrots which can be pressed into the wires of the cage. It is an excellent food for your birds. Another beneficial food is charcoal which is scattered on the floor of the cage for the hens. They spend much time eating and pecking at it. Hens also like soaked seed; not only does this help to vary the diet but it gets them used to the taste of it. This is essential because it is offered when they are feeding young.

With canary seed constantly rising in price it is much too expensive to waste so I have ceased to use canary mixture in the seed hoppers. Instead I put plain canary seed in the hoppers and condition seed and wild seed on the floor of the cage. It is surprising how much time the birds spend picking it over instead of sitting on the perch looking bored.

COMPARING RESULTS

A couple of years ago, in conversation with a friend, he asked me how many youngsters I had bred. I replied 'sixty' and he told me that he had reared fifty-six. However, when we compared notes we found that he had used twenty-four hens, some of which had laid three rounds of eggs.

I had only used eleven hens in the first round and six hens in the second round because part way through the second round I had been ill and my wife had not the time to spend caring for the birds. There was, therefore, a big difference from a productivity point of view between my friend's fifty-six and my sixty!

BIRDROOMS

Canaries are, of course, kept and bred by non-exhibitors as well as keen fanciers who show their birds. During the past forty-eight years I have visited many kinds of birdrooms. One I remember in particular was an old air-raid shelter in the backyard of a terraced house. It had been converted into a very nice little birdroom which contained half-a-dozen pairs of birds.

I have also seen canaries kept in a cellar adapted as a birdroom, in some very nice wooden structures in fanciers' gardens, as well as in brick-built rooms complete with double-glazing and the floors covered with smart-looking tiles.

Birdroom materials

My present birdroom is built with bricks, but my previous birdrooms have been made of timber. It has been my experience that the most satisfactory form of a canary room is one made from timber. There are two very good reasons. In our autumns and winters a wooden birdroom has a greatly reduced air and moisture content, which induces a dry, warm atmosphere.

Although all the windows in my birdroom are double-glazed, in winter the air inside always feels cold and damp, resulting in much more artificial heating being required than in my previous wooden ones. On the other hand, in summer when we have occasional hot sunshine on the roof, it is always cooler inside the brick birdroom.

The second reason is that a birdroom made of timber never has a cold, damp atmosphere in winter, and it requires very little artificial heating. In winter, should there be a little sunshine for an hour or so, it is surprising just how quickly the temperature inside the birdroom goes up. Since I have had a brick birdroom my Borders are three to four weeks later coming into breeding condition.

It is interesting to know that in Australia some canary birdrooms are constructed of corrugated iron. During the very hot summers, when the temperature is 100^0 F (38^0 C) or more, fanciers hose down their birdroom roofs and sides to reduce the temperature inside.

Positioning

In my opinion, the ideal direction for a birdroom to face is east; it then catches the early morning sunshine and the glass windows pick up the heat of the midday sun. This is particularly applicable in spring when our birds are strict followers of the old saying of early to bed and early to rise.

The value of early morning sunshine can be readily appreciated by the

Figure 10.2 Brick-built birdroom

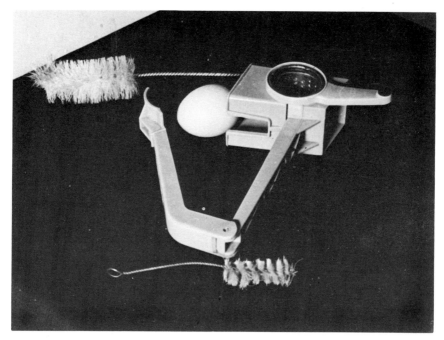

Figure 10.3 Useful birdroom aids — Grater for egg food and two brushes

canaries, and they are then able to follow their natural instincts and, when they have young in the nest, can start feeding from 6 a.m. and continue throughout the day.

Always remember that canaries are sensitive to sudden variations of temperature inside a birdroom. This could be the reason for an indifferent breeding season because at this time a canary is quickly affected by temperature fluctuation.

The question of ventilation is important, as fresh air is very necessary, but a draught can quickly have an adverse effect on a nest of young birds. Therefore, at all times make quite sure that your birds have the benefit of a good fresh air system that is draught-free.

ROUTINE

While on the subject of the well-being of canaries, it is also essential to have a daily routine of hygiene to ensure, for example, that all drinkers are emptied and the insides wiped with a clean cloth.

During my weekly cleaning out of the stock cages, using hot water and a little liquid soap and disinfectant, I always use Dettol. I empty each plastic seed hopper into a fine sieve so that I can remove all the old dust and dirt which has collected during the week in the seed hopper. Before refilling the hopper I thoroughly wipe the inside with a damp cloth which has been moistened with warm water and disinfectant and thoroughly wipe it dry. It is quite true that nothing will adversely affect your bird's health as quickly as drinking infected water, and it is often the cause of an actual illness.

These remarks are particularly applicable where birds are kept in a flight in large numbers, where drinkers are not cleaned daily. Birds in a flight cause bacteria to thrive in their drinking water by dropping into it stale food, decaying greenfood or fouled floor covering from the bottom of the flight. Remember that prevention is much better than cure.

It is a natural thing for all birds to enjoy a bath, so in the morning never hesitate to provide a bath if you see one of your birds trying to bathe in a drinker.

Feather mite

Breeders should always be on the alert for feather mite. There are two signs which can indicate a bird is affected in this way.

1. Rapidly pecking at its feathers all over its body.
2. Baldness at the back of the neck.

If you have a bird affected by mites, catch it up and give it a thorough dusting all over with an insect powder. Work the powder into the bird's feathers with your fingertips. Keating's powder, for example, can still be obtained from chemists.

CHAPTER 11

Food Values

A topical tip for canary fanciers is to offer the birds rose-hip syrup. It is sold by chemists and health food stores and is rich in vitamins. Added to the drinking water at the rate of one tablespoon to one pint of water, it is an easy way of giving the birds some extra vitamins during the winter. Provided in this way two or three times a week, it helps to keep birds in condition.

SWEATING HENS

There has been some discussion in the fancy in the past on the subject of 'sweating hens'. Although this expression is sometimes used, I would question whether, in fact, there is such a thing as a sweating hen. The words describe the state of some hens when they are rearing a brood, when their breast and stomach feathers become damp and matted in appearance. This is not caused by the hen or the young sweating but by the young birds having diarrhoea. The excreta of normal, healthy young is sufficiently solid to enable the hen to keep the inside of the nest clean. This it does for the first seven or eight days by eating the excreta, as at that stage the food is only partly digested.

Fully digested

After the seventh day, food is fully digested by healthy young birds. They pass most of their excreta over the side of the nest, any remaining being thrown out by the hen. When diarrhoea sets in, the excreta becomes so thin and watery that the hen is unable to lift it out of the nest, which becomes damp and wet as a result. The heat of the hen's body draws the dampness into its feathers, making the bird appear to be sweating, which is really not the case. Stop the tendency of diarrhoea in the young so that the excreta becomes normal, and the sweating appearance of the hen will disappear.

Remedy

One of the best remedies is to mix a little raw ground rice or raw arrowroot with the eggfood every time the latter is given. To each teaspoonful of eggfood, add as much ground rice as will cover a one penny piece, or as much arrowroot as will cover a two penny piece. This usually has the effect of bringing things back to normal in a day or two. A pinch of maw seed given daily will also be beneficial.

LINSEED

Linseed, if properly used, is invaluable in the birdroom. Flax or linseed is an annual plant with straight, round stems that are 18 inches to 2 feet (46-61 cm) high and brown near the summit. The leaves, which are very narrow and grow alternately along the stems, are usually about 1 inch (2.5 cm) in length. The flowers have five petals, which are ⅔ inch (1.7 cm) long and a pretty blue colour, and five sepals with three veins.

I am informed that linseed is extensively used in racing stables, where it is given to horses to improve the appearance of their coats, to which it imparts a gloss not easily obtained by other means, and also increases the horses' staying power. It is recommended by many fanciers for producing similar effects on birds. Linseed is very nourishing and is particularly useful during the moult, when it may be given fairly freely. Its properties are demulcent, exercising a highly beneficial effect on the respiratory organs and strengthening the system.

Linseed is invaluable for producing fineness of feather, but, as with other oily seeds, care must be taken to ensure that the proper balance is obtained between fats and carbohydrates. Most important, the seed must be in good condition, clean and sweet, or the birds will suffer from its use. It seems that linseed contains a larger proportion of oily compounds than animals can easily assimilate, so it frequently happens that a portion passes through an animal in an undigested condition. When this occurs, the linseed is, of course, useless as a food, could possibly upset the digestive organs, and might also act as a direct purgative.

Young birds

This is particularly noticeable in the case of young birds. I have heard experienced fanciers express the opinion that it has been the direct cause of death because, in addition to the large quantity of oil, this seed also contains a high percentage of mucilaginous (gummy) matter.

Therefore, linseed should always be administered in comparatively small quantities and mixed with other seeds that are deficient in oily compounds, so as to maintain the balance between the two flesh-forming nutritional elements. Unless this is done, we cannot maintain our birds or any other animals in a vigorous condition. One eminent fancier, who is an authority on bird feeding, states that during his birds' moult he always makes it a practice to mix linseed and canary seed in the proportion of one part linseed to eight parts canary.

During the moult

It has been stated on several occasions that canaries will eat linseed most freely during the early moulting season but some will not touch it at other periods of the year. If this were so, the instinct of the birds would seem to endorse the practice of giving linseed in its various forms for the prevention and cure of the troubles arising from the prevalence of adverse weather.

It is well to remember that the mere presence of the mild, demulcent oil of linseed in a bird's alimentary canal exercises a most soothing effect. It also seems to be of great value when there is a tendency to intestinal irritation.

Nutritional value

Linseed is very nutritious. It is said to contain over 100 grains of protein to the ounce. This means that it is far more nourishing than, for example, wheat, which contains approximately 60 grains, or oats, which contains about 70 grains. Even fresh hens' eggs contain less than 60 grains of protein to the ounce.

So linseed should always be regarded as a highly concentrated food and fed accordingly, because our birds do not like a lot of food fed generously in a concentrated form. Indeed, it is said to be by far the most nourishing of all the seeds in the aviary; therefore, it is far more likely to produce its best effects when given in strict moderation.

It is important to remember that the high praise given to linseed as a food for birds applies only to the very best fresh seed. The grains of these are large and bright and perfectly sweet to the taste with no trace of rancidity.

Incorrectly harvested

When the seed is old or incorrectly harvested, chemical and other changes may have destroyed some of its nutritional value, and since such seed is sometimes offered at tempting prices, it is economy of the worst kind to be led into using it.

BODY FAT

Body fat in a canary serves three purposes; it provides a reserve material to draw from when food is scarce, it provides protection for the oviaries in cold weather and it also provides fat for the egg yolk when the ovaries commence activity. Therefore this fat layer has a direct connection with the oviaries.

FEEDING TIPS

Birds should always be given plenty of fresh air and suitable ventilation and not allowed to eat stale greenfood or stale softfood. Drinking vessels must be washed before being replenished. A hand cloth containing a little disinfectant

144

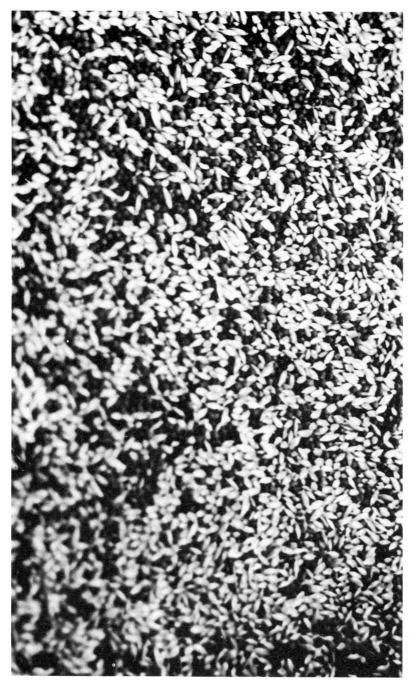

Figure 11.1 A mixture of canary seed and rape seed, which is darker

is admirable for wiping out the drinkers after they have been emptied first thing in the morning.

Fresh canary seed should not be added to seed hoppers until you have blown off the husks from the old seed. At least twice a week, empty the seed hoppers into a sieve to remove dust and husks and replace the seed in the hopper. It is advisable to give hemp seed not more than twice a week, with only a small amount being given at a time.

Canary seed should not be mixed with other seeds, except perhaps a little linseed during the moult; this will prevent wasted seed being scattered on the floor of the cage. Always buy best quality seed (like anything else, you only get what you pay for).

SEED VARIETIES

Most canary enthusiasts know of the great variety of seeds which can be offered to their birds, but few are aware of all the benefits which can be derived by offering the correct foodstuffs at the right time of the year. I shall endeavour to explain the advantages of the various seeds which are readily available to the majority of fanciers.

Canary seed

Canary seed is obtained from the seeding heads of the grass *Phalaris canariensis.* When the husk is removed from fresh, good quality canary seed, the kernel will be found to be a rich walnut brown in colour.

The outer shell is a pale golden colour, with a clean, bright appearance. Dull-looking seed will always open up to show a very light or a very dark-looking skin and this is a sign of bad harvesting or artificial drying.

In my opinion, although this type of seed is usually cheaper to buy, it represents poor economy, as the loss of one good bird can prove far more costly than buying the dearest seed. Remember that, as a rule, you only obtain the quality that you pay for and if a very cheap seed is offered to you, there must be a reason for its low price.

It is generally accepted that large seed is best, but size is not important, as long as the quality is contained within the seed. Canary seed is known to be short of albumenoids (a substance found between the skin and the kernel of the seed) and fats by nearly 10 per cent. At certain times of the year this shortage has to be made up by the use of seeds known to be rich in these particular vitamins.

'Bread and Butter'

In short, canary seed is to canaries what bread and butter is to humans. So you should be prepared to pay for the best.

146

The analysis of canary seed is as follows:

water 13.5 per cent, **albumenoids or proteins** 13.5 per cent, **starch, and other carbohydrates** 51.5 per cent, fats and oils 4.9 per cent and **ash and mineral matter** 2.1 per cent

Therefore, the main food source from canary seed is carbohydrates.

Rape

Rape is a member of the cabbage family, and is extensively grown in England and Germany. It is generally agreed that the German summer rape is by far the best for breeding birds. This is a small reddish-brown seed, with a rich, sweet, nutty taste. I always try chewing a little rape seed before I purchase it. If it tastes sweet and nutty, you can be assured that it is in an ideal state to give to your birds.

A very large black rape seed is available to fanciers, which is used by many Roller Canary enthusiasts. Many leading fanciers of my aquaintance use this variety of rape practically all the year round, mixed with various other seeds.

From late January until the end of the breeding season it is soaked and sprouted for use by the feeding hens. As the youngsters are introduced to colour-food many fanciers use crushed rape as the basis of their mixed seed fed in conjunction with the colour-food. The rape is crushed, sprinkled over the food and mixed with a fork.

If used too freely, rape can be the cause of diarrhoea. However, some individuals remain totally unaffected and can be given as much as they like.

The analysis of rape seed is as follows:

water 11.5 per cent, **albumenoids or proteins** 19.4 per cent, **fats and oils** 40.5 per cent, **starches and other carbohydrates** 10.2 per cent, **ash and mineral matter** 3.9 per cent.

It can therefore be seen that the main source of foods obtained from rape seed are fats and oils.

Blue Maw

Blue Maw is produced from the poppy plant and it is poppy seed. Contrary to popular belief, maw seed contains no opium at all. Opium is obtained from unripe seed capsules. It is grown in many parts of the world.

In many respects maw is the most valuable seed available to the Fancy. Some of us sprinkle it in the sand or wood shavings on the floor of the cage to teach youngsters to pick up their own food in the final stages of weaning.

Out of the breeding season resting birds will benefit from a small amount of the seed on the bottom of their cage, as this is a good way to keep them occupied besides being good for them. No other seed is as good for alleviating both constipation and a looseness of the bowels.

I consider maw seed essential when preparing a mixture of condition seed for the birds. The oil from this seed is very nourishing and is as sweet to a bird's taste as good quality olive oil.

The analysis of maw seed is as follows:

water 14.5 per cent, **albumenoids or proteins** 17.5 per cent, **fats and oils** 40 per cent, **starches and other carbohydrates** 2 per cent, **ash and mineral matter** 6 per cent.

Maw seed is also recognised as being beneficial in preventing aviary-bred youngsters from 'going light'. In my experience, if you feed young birds bread and milk with a liberal sprinkling of maw seed, you will find that many youngsters will make a complete and speedy recovery from apparently 'going light'.

Lettuce seed

Lettuce seed is, in my opinion, one of the finest seeds available. There are several varieties, but the white or light-grey seed is the best for feeding to canaries. The seed should be live. This can be proved by soaking it to see if it sprouts. If it does not, it is of no use and should be discarded. It is also very helpful during the breeding season.

It has a definite purgative action and produces a cooling effect on the bloodstream. It can also help reduce weight. It is highly valued as a cure for 'wheeziness' and vocal problems which canaries experience from time to time.

Lettuce seed is extremely rich in iron and thus is of great value for keeping the blood in a healthy condition. Among the constituents of lettuce are 37 per cent **potash,** 7 per cent **soda,** 14 per cent **lime** and 6 per cent **magnesia.**

Gold of pleasure

Gold of pleasure, or 'false flax' as it is sometimes called, is a member of the cabbage family and is similar in properties to charlock, rape, turnip and radish.

Many older fanciers claim its use tightens and glosses the feathers in the latter stages of the moult and gives the feathers that all-important sheen and appearance. The seed is also claimed to be second to none for bringing hens into breeding condition.

It is a very oily seed and is a very rich gold colour when fully ripe. It's shape is small and round, being only slightly larger than maw seed. It contains a great deal of sulphur in an assimilable state, which is of great medicinal value. However, care should be taken not to over-feed it.

Teazle

Teazle is mostly grown in France, although I know of several canary enthusiasts who grow it in their gardens quite successfully. Teazle is of great value as a food for canaries which have been over-fed on hemp or linseed. It is extremely rich in assimilable nitrogenous matter and is highly nutritious without containing the oily fats of some seeds.

Most experts claim it is an essential ingredient in any mixture of condition

Figure 11.2 Plantain

seed. If my supplier has not included much in his mixture due to the price, I always add a little teazle before feeding it to the birds.

Readily consumed
It is also very readily consumed by feeding hens when it has been soaked or it is just beginning to sprout and, before the second world war, I had hens successfully rear nests on nothing but soaked teazle and bread and milk.

Niger

Niger is a relation of the sunflower. Most of the world's supply is grown in northern India. Unfortunately, the price has greatly increased over the past few years, and even at the higher cost, supplies are not always available. The main purpose of growing niger is to produce lamp oil and good seed is known to produce as much as 40 per cent oil when it is crushed. In order to be of fit quality for consumption by canaries, niger should be jet black in colour, clean and unbroken and very shiny.

Niger is easily broken in transit due to its length and, in this state, it can be most harmful to our birds, due to the oil content of the seed becoming rancid when seeds are damaged.

The feeding of good quality niger to hen canaries during the winter months and at the start of the breeding season is most beneficial. I scatter it on the floor of the flight cages containing the resting hens and I watch them for hours searching through the wood shavings, picking out the niger seed and eating it. At the same time I also include a handful of charcoal.

The analysis of niger seed is as follows:

water 8.5 per cent, **albumenoids and proteins** 17.5 per cent, **fats and oils** 33 per cent, **starches and carbohydrates** 15.5 per cent and **ash or mineral matter** 7 per cent.

Shepherd's purse

Shepherd's purse is of far greater use to the bird fancier than perhaps some people appreciate. In all stages of its growth it is perfectly safe to use, even for youngsters which have just been weaned.

It is to be found growing wild in many parks, and on allotments. It grows between 16-18 inches (41-46 cm) in height and the seed is contained within purse-like pods which are found in considerable numbers at the end of each stalk.

Feeding hens will readily take these stems when they are ripe or even in a half ripe state, and will extract the tiny seeds. If they are not fully ripe, they will be white in colour and very succulent. Several weeds resemble shepherd's purse, but few, if any, are as good as this weed. In terms of nutritional value it is hard to surpass.

Hemp

Hemp is grown extensively in southern Europe and the U.S.A. The plant is quite large, growing to 5-6 ft (1.5-1.8 m) in height. The colour of good quality seed varies from light to dark olive green. Hemp of a light green colour is generally unripe and that of a very dark grey shade, which is very light in weight, is old and useless.

Good seed is very nourishing, although it can be fattening and, therefore, it is more suitable as a winter food than one for all the year round.

Soaked or cracked
Hemp is acknowledged by many breeders as an essential addition to the birds' diet during the breeding season. Some fanciers crack the hemp and others

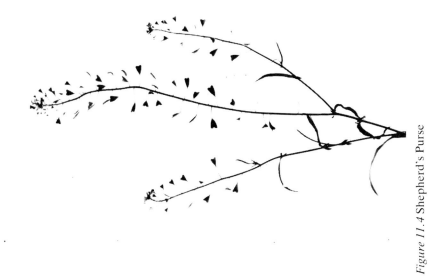

Figure 11.4 Shepherd's Purse

Figure 11.3 Persicaria

soak it until it is about to sprout and then give it in limited quantities to the feeding hens. Sprouted hemp is an excellent food for breeding canaries.

The analysis of this seed is as follows:

water 12 per cent, **albumenoids and proteins** 16.5 per cent, **fats and oils** 32 per cent, **starch and other carbohydrates** 16 per cent, **ash or minerals** 4.3 per cent.

Persicaria

Persicaria is another excellent wild seed. It is often seen growing between rows in potato fields, with its reddish-white flowers and similarly coloured seeds.

If a handful of this is sprinkled on the cage floor when the birds are moulting, you will find that they will spend a good deal of time picking it over.

Figure 11.5 Seeding Dock; excellent food for moulting canaries

CHAPTER 12

Making Your Own Softfood

IMPORTANCE OF FOOD VALUES

If a bird is to have a really successful show season it is essential to maintain the quality and sheen of its feathers; to achieve this a fairly extensive knowledge of the food requirements of a canary is necessary. The properties and food values of seeds can be divided into four groups which are as follows:

(a) composition;

(b) digestible nutrients;

(c) starch equivalents;

(d) nutrient ratio (so that a comparison can be made between different foods).

When food is analysed it is necessary to know the content of the following:

(a) water;

(b) ash;

(c) proteins;

(d) fat content;

(e) fibre and roughage.

It is true that different foods when fed to canaries have varying degrees of digestibility than when fed to other animals. However, it is interesting to note that a bird's powers of digestion are greater than those of larger domesticated animals. It is also interesting to know that if a farmer wishes to fatten his stock he will offer a great deal of fat producing constituents and only a limited amount of protein.

Fattening constituents

On the other hand, if his hens are to lay the maximum number of eggs, he will be careful to feed them a lot of protein and a relatively small amount of fattening constituents. This type of diet should be fed to all developing young canaries.

One of the most important characteristics of any food, which its appearance cannot show us, is how palatable it is and this can only be found out by offering it to the birds. It will be found that most birds have very strong likes and dislikes for certain seeds, greenfoods, and so on. For this reason, it is sometimes advisable not to feed your birds only on what the analysts recommend, but to also feed a little of whatever they like best.

The nutrient requirements of cage birds vary considerably according to the species. For example, a finch takes only the kernel, while pigeons and doves swallow the husks as well as the seed.

Generally, canaries require food containing the following; **moisture, protein, fat,** and **carbohydrates.** Below is a list of the essential mineral properties which are necessary for birds, and the foods which contain them.

Calcuim found in cabbage, lettuce, spinach, watercress, dandelion and egg yolk.
Magnesium found in cabbage, lettuce, spinach and apple.
Potassium found in lettuce, watercress, and soaked oats.
Iodine found in cabbage, lettuce and carrots.
Chlorine found in cabbage, lettuce, spinach and egg white.
Iron found in lettuce, spinach, dandelion and egg yolk.
Sodium found in cabbage, lettuce, spinach, dandelion, apple and carrot.
Phosphorus found in cabbage, lettuce, spinach, watercress, apple, egg yolk and sprouts.
Silicon found in cabbage, lettuce, spinach, dandelion and apple.

It is unreasonable to expect any canary to do well if you only feed it canary and rape seed all the time. No seed exists which, in itself, contains a full range of food values. I know of canary breeders who put only mixed millet in the food hoppers and, in addition, daily give a little canary and rape and a small amount of mixed condition seed.

My basic seed mixture comprises canary and rape mixed to a ratio 4:1, to which I add a little niger, linseed and small hemp. I alter this basic food according to the month and the time of the year.

Charcoal

In my book, *The Border Canary* (Saiga Publishing, 1981) I have stated that canaries do not require the use of grit to enable them to digest their food. This I know is a matter of opinion and perhaps I can explain why I have reached my decision.

The first thing that a canary does on picking up in its beak any form of seed, canary, rape, or dock, for example, is to remove the husks. This is done in less than one second. The reason why a canary is able to de-husk seed so efficiently is because the bird's beak is its actual teeth. Once the seed has been de-husked, a canary, or other seedeater, is quite able to digest it while it is in the crop, and the assistance of grit during this process is, in my opinion, not required in any way.

On the other hand, those species which pick up seed and corn and immediately swallow it, do require grit. These include such birds as pheasants and quail. As these birds do not de-husk seeds and grain, the grit is necessary to assist in its breakdown. Referring to the subject of grit, N.W. Wodan writes:

The function of grit, and the need for supplying it, are topics of continual debate. Generally speaking it may be stated that grit is employed by the bird to facilitate the trituration of food that is not already ground, e.g. whole grains or seeds. In the case of finches which de-husk their food before swallowing it, however, there are many instances in which grit is withheld without apparent harm.

A probable second function of grit is that of so mixing with the food mass that it separates it and prevents it from forming large, coalescent lumps, and at the same time permits the digestive juices to flow freely among it. Blount suggests that grit may, by helping to distend the gizzard, play a part in determining the call for more grit, i.e. the greater the distention the less the demand.

The function of grit in grinding or in separating the food mass depends upon its hardness. Limestone grit tends to dissolve in the gizzard and is therefore not a complete substitute for a hard, insoluble grit. It does, however, supply calcium or lime — sometimes, perhaps, to local excess. There is growing evidence that, at least in young gramnivorous birds, an alkaline reaction in the upper part of the alimentary tract may favour certain types of infection.

The recommendation of choice, where grit is indicated, is to provide a hard, insoluble grit and to ensure that the diet otherwise is not deficient in lime. For larger birds at least, granite is preferable to quartz or flint, which tends to fissure into knife-like particles.

What is essential for canaries is charcoal. Not only does it assist with the digestion of the food in the crop, but it also contains various important trace elements.

From a bonfire

You can acquire granulated charcoal from most seed merchants, or, if you have had a bonfire in the garden to dispose of an old tree trunk, when the fire has been completely extinguished the charred remains of the wood can be collected and kept in a plastic bag. A teaspoonful can be fed once a week to each of the canaries, both cocks and hens. The only time that I withold charcoal from my Borders' stock cages is during the show season, and then only for the birds which I intend to exhibit.

During my visits to canary breeders in Victoria and South Australia in 1978 and 1980 I noticed that many fanciers were also feeding charcoal to their canaries. All of the main cities of Australia are either actually situated on or are very near to clean sandy beaches, and I noticed that in these areas the floors of cages and flights were covered with a mixture of this sand and shell grit. I noticed, too, that at some Australian canary shows the floors of the various show cages had to be covered with shellgrit and not canary seed as is the case in the United Kingdom.

Here, it is generally accepted that the floors of stock cages are covered with either sawdust or wood shavings, but that is not the case with the majority of fanciers in Australia and on the continent of Europe. In Spain and Italy, for example, many fanciers use newspaper as a cage floor covering, which is replaced at least every other day. Their standard of hygiene would appear to be higher than is the case of some canary breeders in the United Kingdom.

Once the show season is over I give all my hens a liberal supply of charcoal. During the winter months I make a particular point of scattering the charcoal on the floor of the flight cages, as it helps to keep the birds active and interested.

I am a firm believer in feeding a little sprouted seed throughout the year, as this contains many more vitamins than plain, hard seed. All these play an essential part in ensuring that my stock remains fit and well.

Chicken pellets

It is surprising the number of birds kept in captivity which will eat insects. When I first visited Australia in 1978, I was surprised at the number of canary breeders who used ground-up chicken pellets as the basic ingredient of their softfood and they had all enjoyed a good breeding season.

Their reason for using these pellets was that millions of pounds had been spent on researching food containing suitable vitamins for poultry over the past two decades and that, in many respects, the digestive systems of chickens have much in common with those of canaries.

Another home-made canary softfood which the fanciers in Victoria use comprises two parts oatmeal, two parts pea meal, one part rice powder, one part honey, one part sterilised bonemeal, one part fish meal, one part grated suet and a little salt. All the contents are thoroughly mixed together.

Seed merchants

Another significant difference between Australia and the United Kingdom is that there are few seed merchants in Australia. Australian canary fanciers purchase most of their requirements from their local cage bird societies, which all have a seed and accessory counter, which opens for business at all club meetings. Some of the larger clubs will even deliver in bulk if an order is placed. This not only offers members cheaper seed with no carriage costs involved, but at the same time it is a source of income for the local society. Exactly the same system operates in Spain.

Shell-grit

Many fanciers firmly believe that canaries eat shell-grit to assist their digestive system by grinding the seed with its sharp edges. This line of thought is only partly true. Grit can help in this way, but this is only a minor process, as it is the acids in the bird's digestive system which are capable of breaking down a canary's food into body-building nourishment, without any grinding whatsoever. A canary's food is broken down into small pieces before being eaten, otherwise the bird would have difficulty in swallowing it.

In my opinion, birds are inclined to eat grit because of a natural impulse and they can obtain a small amount of minerals from it, thus aiding feather formation. I have not fed my canaries any grit for the past 20 years. In my opinion, provided that you offer your birds a properly balanced diet (according to the month of the year), the bird's digestive system will not require grit.

Figure 12.1 Various feeders

Figure 12.2 Teazle heads and Plantain

On the other hand, calcium is one of the most important elements in the make-up of a bird, as a large amount is actually discharged in the bird's droppings and, of course, this has to be replaced. I always ensure that my birds have plenty of cuttlefish bone.

Lime water

For those of you who are firm believers in offering grit, I suggest that you add a little lime to the drinking water. Once a bird has got used to this, it will not visit the shell-grit container to any great extent and it will drink much more of the lime water. This would appear to satisfy the need for minerals.

Those of you who do not have the time to spend with your birds, particularly during the winter months, will find that they either aimlessly sit on the perch at one end of the cage or just hop about the cage floor looking bored with nothing to do. I suggest that you do two things to alleviate this particular mental attitude of the birds.

Add a little lime to their drinking water and scatter a handful of charcoal on the floor of the cage. I have used charcoal in this manner for the past 45 years. Even before then I can remember being told by an old fancier that charcoal is 'the source of life' for cage birds and I have practised this ever since.

After only a couple of days you will see quite a change in your birds' attitude; they will be much more active, their feathers will be tighter and they will appear to be enjoying life. The correct proportion is a teaspoonful of slack lime to a gallon of water and this should be offered three times a week. It can also be beneficial during the moulting season.

It does not follow that lime will supply everything that is needed during the moult, so that your birds reach peak condition, as there are many other necessary minerals.

However, if you take care to feed the moulting birds on the greenfoods listed earlier in this chapter you should be well satisfied with their condition and colour at the end of the moult. It is well-known that all animals suffer if they have a shortage of phosphorous and that many illnesses can be attributed to this deficiency.

The vast majority of birds do very much better if they can regularly sun themselves. The health-giving properties of sunlight are not only due to its actual warmth, but also to the beneficial effects of the ultra-violet rays to which the birds are exposed.

REGULAR FEEDING

As I have stated in previous chapters, the regular feeding of the right greenfood cannot be over-emphasised, if the birds are to remain in good health and good feather and are to have a reasonable chance of rearing their young.

There is no reason why there should be any shortage of greenfood, irrespective of the weather, because, in any event, it can simply be replaced by sprouted wheat, rye, barley or oats. These sprouted seeds should be offered when they have grown to about half an inch long.

Sprouting seeds

If you have a flight or aviary try sprouting your seeds on the floor. Place an 8 inch (20 cm) square piece of turf on the ground and watch your birds for half an hour — their reactions will more than thank you for having done so. When the sprouted seed has been partially eaten, the turf should be replaced, and allowed to recover its growth in the garden in the normal way.

If you live in a town, I suggest that you obtain two or three seed boxes and sow a mixture of grass seed, millet and condition seed. You will be amazed at just how much your canaries will enjoy the result when it has grown to about half an inch or so in height.

Early spring greenfood

In order to maintain a good source of early spring greenfood, you should rake over an area of about two square yards of soil and at the end of August or early September scatter over the fine soil three or four handfuls of black rape and gently rake the seed into the soil. By the time April arrives you will have some well-grown rape plants, the young leaves of which make an excellent greenfood for canaries.

Cuttlefish bone

I have previously explained the value of providing an adequate supply of cuttlefish bone. When my hens are busy completing their nests, I take a really sharp knife and peel pieces of cuttlefish off the bone in the same way as you peel an apple. I place them in a softfood dish for the birds.

You will quickly see that the hens come and pick out quite large pieces of the peeled cuttlefish bone, leaving behind them a hole in the cuttlefish bone in the shape of their beak. You can, if you so wish, grate the cuttlefish bone and mix it with the softfood, just before giving it to your canaries.

Rearing food mixture

A good rearing food which is well worth trying is as follows; 8 oz. bread-crumbs or crushed biscuits, 2 oz. ground-up linseed, 3 oz. finely ground oatmeal, 3 oz. ground rye, 4 oz. powdered loaf sugar and 2 oz. crushed hemp seed (free of husks). Mix well together using one large, sieved hard-boiled egg when being fed to the young, and add a little maw seed.

This type of softfood is invaluable for canaries and can be fed to great advantage during the winter months. You will find that canaries quickly acquire a liking for it. A teaspoonful of this offered every other day is adequate for any birds when not breeding, keeping them in a good, healthy condition.

During the breeding season you should continue to use this softfood, but

Figure 12.3 Nest-box. *Courtesy* Ponderosa of Cheltenham

in larger quantities. The only precaution to take is to ensure that it does not become sour. This can be avoided by keeping it in an air-tight tin in a cool place and only adding the hard-boiled egg to the softfood when it is being fed to the birds.

Cake

When I was a boy, fanciers' wives used to prepare a baked cake for the birds, which was easy to make and in those days cost little. To make this cake, first take 10 medium-sized eggs, break and separate the yolks from the whites, and put them into individual dishes. Add to the yolks 9 oz. of sugar and 12 oz. of plain flour. Take a lemon or an orange, extract all the juice from it and pour it into the flour and egg mixture. Stir it together briskly for about five minutes and add the egg white, stirring well.

This mixture will make two cakes of about 9 inch (23 cm) diameter. Before putting the mixture into the two cake tins, make sure the bottoms and the sides have been well greased and lightly dusted with flour.

Using a medium hot oven, the cakes should be cooked for about 50-55 minutes. When they have been cooked and while they are still warm, cut them up into half inch slices and leave them to dry out. You might have to complete the drying out process by returning them to a cool oven for a while.

When quite cold, put the cake through a mincer, until it becomes a powdery mixture. Store it in an air-tight container. When required turn out the amount you intend to use and soften it with milk, but only feed it to the birds crumbly. If, however, you want to use it as a cleanser for your birds' bowels, you should feed it to them in a very sloppy state.

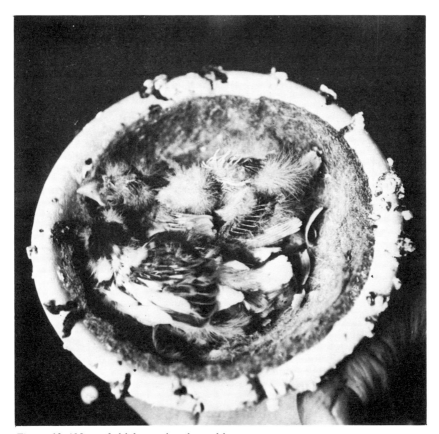

Figure 12.4 Nest of chicks at nine days old

CHAPTER 13

Canaries in Australia

During my trips to Australia in 1978, 1980 and 1982, I visited breeders of all varieties of canaries who lived in South Australia, Victoria, New South Wales and Queensland and, during these three visits, I have travelled some 95,000 miles by air, besides being taken thousands of miles by road.

AUSTRALIAN BREEDS

The Australians breed and exhibit all the main exhibition canaries we see in the U.K. except for the Old Varieties, but this is more than counter-balanced by large numbers of **Australian Plainhead Canaries.** This is a canary developed by Australian fanciers, and is only to be found there. Many of the best Australian Plainheads which I saw exhibited were self Cinnamons which excelled in colour and feather, like our canaries of 30 years ago. The Plainhead is not as big as a Norwich, being some 6 inches (15 cm); it has a bold head, distinct neck, flat back, perfectly clear eye, fairly long straight legs, and is much more active in the show cage than a Norwich, more like the Border. Considering that it is quite a large canary, its feather quality is equal to that of a Gloster. These canaries remind me of the type of Norwich shown in drawings of a hundred years ago, but they are not colour fed, being bred for richness of colour like a Border is.

Leading the world

The world's leading country for the breeding of Type Canaries is, without any doubt, the United Kingdom. During the last decade it has been my good fortune to visit breeders and shows in several European countries, the Far East, Australia and America, and it has delighted me to see the improvements being made in these countries by the breeders of Type Canaries. I have found that, generally speaking, the different breeders in these countries have fully accepted the British standards of excellence. Where this is not so, the difference is only a small one.

Such is the case with Borders in the U.S.A., but even there, if a really outstanding British type Border were to be exhibited, its sheer excellence

162

would ensure that it took the award for best Border. I feel sure that it will not be long before American fanciers accept the British standard. At the present time they breed a 5 inch (13 cm) Border with very little back; it is finer in the head than the British Border.

I have come across but a single example of a Type Canary with major alterations to the British standard, and that was when I was invited to judge at the 1980 Australian Interstate Canary championship show held in Dandenong in the state of Victoria. At this show there were several cases of Carophyll Red fed Borders. The reason for this is that in the city of Sydney classes for colour-fed Borders are an accepted thing. Sydney was the only place I know of in Australia where Borders are actually colour-fed. I dislike their appearance and I did not hesitate to tell my Australian co-judge that I thought so; needless to say, I was not invited to judge the Colour-fed Borders.

Speaking of Type Canaries, I have found that the best Lizard Canaries outside the United Kingdom are in northern Spain. The failing of those birds is in their spangles. When I first visited Australia in 1978 I found that all their Lizards had some light feathering on their bodies, flights or tails, the reason being that only a few years ago pure Lizard Canaries were almost extinct in Australia; in 1982 they had made great improvements in the quality of their Lizards.

Light feathering

In April 1980 I was most pleasantly surprised to see the great improvement which had been made in the young Lizards, many of which were showing a very small amount of light feathering, like spots on the body, or only an odd light feather in flights or tail. There had also been a distinct improvement in their spanglings and rowing and I predict that by 1984 the Australian Lizard will be a credit to them, possibly even the best outside the U.K.

Borders

I have now judged Borders from every state in Australia, plus three all-Border international shows in the U.K. I could quite easily have selected an Australian all-Border team which at least would come a very good second in any U.K. all-Border contest.

Australia is such a vast continent, with its major cities being between 500 and 2,000 miles apart, that it was no surprise to find a little difference in the opinions in the different states regarding type. Australian Borders excel in quality. Their biggest weakness is in Self Greens and Cinnamons; these, I regret to say, look like a long-term problem as no new blood can be taken into Australia.

Glosters

Australian Gloster Canaries, especially the Green Consorts, are very close to the English standards. Most of the states in Australia have fully accepted our

Figure 13.1 A 1900 Border

Gloster standard and breed closely to it; only the New South Wales Gloster Club has recently drawn up a standard of its own.

The Australian Glosters are small and compact with plenty of daylight between the body and the perch, a short compact tail and broad head, with plenty of feather. They are very much like the late Fred Bryant's Glosters of the 1950s, except that their Coronas are not as precise in the shape of the crest.

Societies

Every Australian Canary Society sends each paid-up member a Newsletter each month, which can have as many as thirty pages. The Aussies have a great sense of humour as the following extract from one of their Newsletters will show:

> **We give below the following tips on 'How to ruin your Club'!**
> 1. **Don't attend the meetings.**
> 2. **If you do — then come late.**
> 3. **When you attend, sit at the back and talk to the person next to you about the weather or football.**

4. Never accept office. It's much easier to criticise than do anything.
5. If asked by the Chairman for your opinion, just tell him you have nothing to say, and then, after the meeting tell everyone how things should have been done.
6. Hold back your subscription as long as you possibly can.
7. Don't bother about getting new members — let someone else do it. After all there's plenty of others who have time for that sort of thing.
8. In short, do nothing more than is absolutely necessary. But when other members roll up their sleeves and do the lot, howl like mad about how the organisation is being run by a clique.

The Australians say, feed your canaries for natural colour

We must try to breed all types of canaries which have natural colour. A fancier cannot for a moment expect rich, natural-coloured chicks from parents that are pale and of poor quality feather. They feed their birds a lot of dandelion leaves, from spring to late autumn; they say it acts both as a tonic and keeps their birds fit and well, and that it also enhances natural depth of colour during the moult. All their canary fanciers use it, New Colours, colour-fed birds and non-colour-fed alike.

Australian dandelions grow differently to ours; they have a shorter length of leaf which grows flat along the ground. They also split open the root and feed that as well. Here, we feed the large, fluffy seeding heads to our feeding hens, but the Australian seeding head is less than a third of the size of ours, and I have not seen it being fed in any birdroom which I visited.

Australia imports all its rape seed and regulations state that it has to be heavily disinfected. As a result, canaries will not eat it. To offset this, large quantities of canary seed are grown locally, and this forms a relatively cheap basic food for the birds.

Many Australian fanciers make up their own softfood, usually comprising the following items: crushed fine arrowroot biscuits, high protein baby food, maw seed, castor sugar, and hard boiled egg, which are thoroughly mixed together with the aid of a fork, no other moisture being used. As neither teazle or hemp seed are grown or imported, four or five different types of millet seed are soaked in water for twenty-four hours, then thoroughly rinsed and left to sprout, when they are fed to breeding hens, who very readily eat every sprouting seed.

Reasonable pairs

The price of breeding stock varies according to the type of Canary, but the ones in most demand such as Borders, New Colours, Australian Plainheads, Yorkshires, Norwich and Lizards, cost from £25 per pair, and for that money their quality would be better than many similar kinds in the U.K. This I found applied to South Australia, Victoria, New South Wales and Queensland.

While at Willunga, South Australia, I saw some really excellent Border show cages being made by a young chap, John Horner, who was blind; his wife was the Secretary of the State Border Fancy Club.

Figure 13.2 Typical Australian canary flight

Rose-hip syrup

A typical tip of theirs to fanciers whose birds have lost their vital sparkle, is to give their birds rose-hip syrup — it is sold by most chemists and health food shops. Added to the drinking water at the rate of one tablespoon to one pint of water, and providing that this is done two or three times a week, it helps to keep the birds in condition.

Yorkshires

Australian Yorkshires closely follow the U.K. standard of excellence; they look for feather quality, and many of these birds carry Cinnamon blood. The outstanding Yorkshire breeder is Stan Nicholls of Victoria; his birds, if exhibited in the U.K., would be difficult to beat. Stan is the masseur to the Australian tennis team which plays in the U.K. and, while here, Stan takes the opportunity to visit many of our leading Yorkshire breeders, so he knows the standard of U.K. birds.

Birdrooms

The average Australian canary room is larger than ours in the U.K., and each room will contain at least two indoor flights, which will at least measure 7 feet long, 4 feet wide, and 7 feet high (2.1 x 1.2 x 2.1m). The perches will be 6 feet (1.8m) from the floor and are staggered so that no bird can sit directly above another one; the seed dishes and drinks are above floor level. At one birdroom I visited in Victoria there were some 600 new Colours, which included not only Reds but also many of the different colour mutations which we have in Europe. In quite a lot of birdrooms there were flowering plants, and in one a goldfish pond in the floor. It was nice to see how clean and natural were the canaries' feathers. A lot of fanciers never even needed to hand-wash a bird before exhibiting it.

Most Australian fanciers have large gardens, which they call 'back yards', and these usually contain trees and shrubs, all of which help to provide natural shade for a canary breeding room. There the birdrooms are either constructed of wood or, in some cases, galvanised corrugated iron.

False roof
Many structures have a false roof which allows the free passage of air between the two layers, which results in cool conditions during the very hot summers.

In cases where mosquitoes could be a source of worry, the Australians use an inner spring-closing door clad in very fine gauze. Such material allows a passage of air to enter, but not mosquitoes. A similar type of frame is fitted to the windows. It is easy to see why Australian fanciers' birds seldom succumb to canary pox.

We have our cold winter months to contend with, it is true, but this is more than offset by the moderate summers with no extremes in temperature or mosquitoes to contend with. I think that we should put far less blame on the weather for lack of success during the breeding season.

CHAPTER 14

Canary Ailments

To me one of the most frustrating things about canary keeping is the very limited written instructive literature which is available to canary fanciers about diseases and illnesses of canaries. Actually, canaries are just like human beings in that they are subject to many illnesses. The average fancier just does not have the technical knowledge to enable him to define just what illness a sick bird has. Even if he correctly guesses just what it might be, then has he the knowledge of the correct remedy to apply?

FUNCTION OF THE LUNGS

Birds live their lives with an intensity as extreme as their brilliant colours and their vivid songs. Their body temperatures are regularly as high as 105^0 - 110^0 F (41-43^0 C) and anyone who has watched a bird at close range must have seen how its whole body vibrates with the furious pounding of its pulse. Such an engine must operate at forced draught – and that is exactly what a bird does. The bird's in-drawn breath not only fills its lungs but also passes on through the myriads of tiny tabules into air sacs that fill every space in the bird's body not occupied by vital organs. Furthermore, the air sacs connect with many of the bird's bones which are not filled with marrow, as animals' bones are, but are hollow. These reserve air 'tanks' provide fuel for the birds intensive life, and at the same time add to its buoyancy in flight.

HEPATITUS

This disease primarily affects the liver and the kidneys, and is caused by either contaminated drinking water or by the bird eating oily seeds which have picked up the virus. Seeds such as niger, which is a long, very oily seed, may carry the virus, and if the husk becomes damaged its 35% of oil content can soon go off. If you suspect that one of your birds has developed hepatitus, catch it up and examine its body by blowing the feathers apart. If its stomach is purple-blue colour then it is almost certain that the bird has a complaint related to the liver and kidneys, possibly hepatitus.

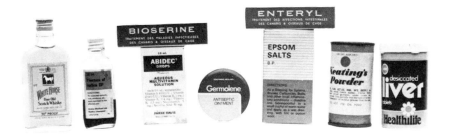

Figure 14.1 Some useful medicines

Treatment
Place the bird in a hospital cage which has a temperature of 85⁰· F (29⁰· C), give a general antibiotic in its drinking water, such as **auramicin** or **terramicin;** feed a teaspoonful of both softfood and sprouted seed, also canary seed and rape. The course of action should be; warmth, rest, a good balanced diet, and the antibiotic should do the rest. A week of this treatment should bring a big improvement. Gradually reduce the temperature of the hospital cage.

RESPIRATORY COMPLAINTS

With some fanciers' stock these problems are fairly common because, in my opinion, good management is not being applied. Canaries are very sensitive to draughts and dampness, so always ensure that your birdroom is free of draughts, but the birdroom or shed must have a supply of fresh air. Where a birdroom is constructed of wood, then care should be taken to insulate it against frost and excessive high temperatures. We should always remember that when a canary becomes ill the very first thing that will happen to the bird is an immediate fall in its temperature, so irrespective of what is the cause of the illness, the first thing to do is place the bird in a hospital cage which has a temperature of some 85⁰ F (29⁰ C), and put five drops of glycerine in its water and mix well together.

PNEUMONIA

This complaint is generally the result of the bird having been exposed to a draught, especially if it has been at a show near an outside door which was in constant use. Canaries with this complaint will have rapid breathing and appear to be gasping for breath.

169

Treatment

Add an antibiotic **(terramicin)** to its drinking water and feed it easily digested fresh food, such as bread soaked in milk and glucose well sprinkled with maw seed, and sprouted seed. Three days of this treatment should see the bird back to normal. If the bird hardly uses its drinker, catch it up once every hour and put five drops of its water down the back of its throat. The bird should be kept in a hospital cage.

ENTERITIS

The symptoms of the complaint are the bird passing frequent very loose droppings. In very bad cases its droppings are in liquid form, and the vent and its feathers will be soiled. The cause could be stale softfood, contaminated drinking water, or infected greenfood.

Treatment

The first thing to do is to put the bird in a thoroughly disinfected cage (in particular the perches). Wash and dry the drinker and refill it with a mixture of water and whisky, and remove **all** forms of greenfood. The bird will obviously feel ill and will crouch on the perch, and have a loss of appetite. Catch up the bird three times a day and put five drops of whisky and water down the back of the throat; in the evening give the bird three drops of castor oil. Remove the seed hopper and feed the bird on a good quality softfood to which you have added hard-boiled egg, maw seed and **finely ground-up** rice and arrowroot, all well mixed together thoroughly. **Do not forget,** keep the bird in a warm cage. If the complaint is a very bad one then you should put **terramicin** in the water for three days.

INDIGESTION

Canaries do have indigestion and this is indicated when the bird vomits its food, causing it to spread about the cage as it jerks its head.

Treatment

To treat the bird you should limit the amount of its hard seed, give it bread soaked in milk and glucose, and scatter on it maw seed. If you add five drops of syrup of buckthorn to its drinking water the bird should soon be back to normal; on the second day, feed a **teaspoonful** of sprouted seed.

ASTHMA

Birds which have asthma have difficulty in breathing; it can often be the result of a neglected cold. Once a canary starts to breathe heavily it should receive attention. Give the bird a little eggfood and bread and milk, and add a little glycerine and honey, mixed well together, in its drinking water. A bird which has a severe attack of asthma is best put down.

COLDS

A bird suffering from a cold will show this condition by sitting in a crouching position on the perch, with its feathers ruffled out, indicating a loss of body temperature.

Treatment

Put it immediately in a hospital cage, give it a little softfood, and add five drops of glycerine in its water. After three days it should be back to normal.

THRUSH

This disease primarily affects the mouth; if you are hand feeding young ones in the nest they can quickly be affected. It has a greyish white appearance and forms a deposit on the edes of the beak. When hand feeding, it can easily be avoided if you wet your fingers and wipe the edge of the beak after each feed. Adult birds having this complaint are quickly cured of it if you put permanganate of potash in the drinking water.

EYE DISEASES

Birds which are affected by a cold or foreign matter in their eye should be caught up and the affected eye washed in a solution of boracic powder and water with the aid of cotton wool. Then wipe the eye dry and gently rub in some **Golden Eye ointment,** obtainable from Boots the Chemists. Any form of infection of the eye cannot be better treated than in the way I have described.

FEET AND LEGS

During the breeding season you will find that an occasonal young bird will leave the nest with its rear claw pointing **forward** like its three toes. This is referred to as **slip claw.** In these cases, catch up the young bird, get hold of the

Figure 14.2 Hospital cage

slip claw and **gently** bend it backwards until it touches the the actual leg. Then, holding it in that position, gently tie the claw back to the leg with a soft piece of wool. Leave it like this for two weeks, then remove the wool and you will find that now the rear claw can grip the perch normally. Care should be taken to ensure that thin twig perches are used.

When a bird is four or five weeks old it should grip the perches in a normal way. However, a bird may suddenly be seen sitting on a perch with one rear claw at 90^0 to its leg, thus being unable to grip the perch – this is called **stiff hind claw.** The treatment for this is to remove all perches and cuttlefish bone. Gently massage the joint with olive oil three times a day. On the fourth day, make a perch out of a ¼ inch piece of rope by tying one end of it to the cage front, pull it tight, and then, with the aid of a strong drawing pin, secure it low down, at the back of the cage. This type of perch will encourage the bird to try to grip with the rear claw. After three or four weeks of this treatment you should see a marked improvement in the use of the claw.

SCALY LEGS AND FEET

Some canaries develop ugly scaly legs and feet; in these cases get a tin of **zinc** ointment and mix it thoroughly with a little paraffin oil until you have a soft paste. Then, using your first finger and thumb, rub the mixture well into the scales, twice a day. After a few weeks the scales will gradually fall off.

LOSS OF FEATHERS

This generally occurs at the back of the neck leaving bare skin. In these cases, catch up the bird, bend its head over your thumb and give it a thorough dusting with **Keating's powder,** obtainable from Boots the Chemists. With the bird in your hand, work some Keating's into **all** its feathers with your fingers. A single treatment will kill off all the trouble – feather lice.

USE OF HOSPITAL CAGE

As previously explained, when a bird is ill, its body temperature immediately falls, so all fanciers are advised to have a hospital cage. These are easy to make, as the illustration shows, and will cost very little — **but** it could be the means of saving the life of your most valuable bird.

TOE NAILS

A bird which has very long toe nails is not able to grip the perch properly; if the nails are very long they will have difficulty in releasing the perch. In these cases, catch up the bird, hold it on the palm of your hand, then hold one toe at a time between your first finger and thumb. Look for the vein in the centre of the nail then, using a sharp pair of scissors, cut off the excess nail ⅛ **inch beyond the end of the vein.** Should a nail commence to bleed, then apply **iodine** as this will quickly congeal the blood.

GOING LIGHT

This disease is self-explanatory by its very name; the bird gradually wastes away to a mere skeleton. To a newcomer to the fancy, some birds when they first start to go light, actually appear to eat and drink more. This complaint appears to occur much more frequently among nest feather birds than in adults. Birds with this complaint appear to have their feathers ruffled, and sit huddled in one position. The most vulnerable birds are usually between six and twelve weeks old.

The cause of the complaint is mainly incorrect feeding and lack of proper hygiene; never leave stale or surplus softfood in their cages. The thing to do is to make sure that you feed young canaries a properly balanced and easily digested diet. Make certain that they have ready access to a supply of granulated charcoal which, besides having many different trace elements, also assists in the digestion of food in their crops. I personally never put young birds solely on hard seed until they have completed their moult. Young birds should have **Orovite '7'** in their drinking water every other day until they have completed their moult; it is a soluble multi-vitamin powder, a big point being that the bird will only absorb what it requires.

SIGNS OF HEALTH AND SICKNESS

The body of a canary can give important indications as to its health. The breast should be plump and round but the breast-bone should not be visible. A pointed, outstanding breast-bone indicates a defective system of feeding or the presence of disease.

The abdomen of a healthy cock should be flatter than the breast and a dark flesh colour. In the hen, it should be fuller and, when in breeding condition, rounded with a layer of fat which shows a lighter colour than the cock's. If a canary is out-of-sorts, place it on its back in the palm of your hand. Blowing on the feathers may reveal a brown spot on one or both sides of the abdomen just below the breast. Such spots indicate an infection of the liver and the bird should not be used for breeding.

When a canary is suffering from indigestion, even to the slightest degree, the feathers are not carried smoothly but appear fluffed out, and are not as clean as those of a healthy specimen. Imperfect action of the digestive organs is also indicated when a bird does not de-husk its chief foods – canary and rape seed – properly. Instead, it grinds the seeds and bolts them down. A condition often ensues similar to 'going light'. As symptoms become worse, the bird becomes fluffed up and tends to eat all of the time, as it grows weaker it is unable to eat and so loses weight rapidly.

The use of tonics and medicines ensure that an ailing bird regains its normal, happy state of health, and we are fortunate that a number of different cures are available on the market. Liquid preparations are usually the best as they are easier to administer and are digested quicker than those in powder form. In an emergency a few drops of brandy and water can be put down the bird's throat, and it will act as a wonderful pick-me-up.

Antibiotics obtained only on a veterinary surgeon's prescription, can be used successfully to counteract fungus in chest complaints. Even if these are available, the complaint must be caught in its early stages if a complete cure is to be effected.

DRAUGHTS

While talking about canary ailments, always ensure that your birdroom is free from draughts, especially so when the birds are in the moult, for this is often the reason for a bird 'getting stuck in the moult'. In other words, it starts to moult and then stops.

If this happens you will have to revert to a forcing procedure. This is done by placing a few shreds of the flowers of **saffron** in half a cupful of boiling water, allowing it to stand until the water is cold. The liquid should then be put in the bird's drinking water, and this repeated for three days. During the next few days the bird should recommence its moult in the normal way.

BODY TEMPERATURE

The body temperature of a healthy canary is between 107^0 F and 109^0 F $(42-43^0$ C). A bird controls its body temperature by movement of its feathers. Human beings and horses lose excessive body heat by perspiration of the skin. A dog cannot actually sweat so it loses excessive body heat by panting; the air moving over the moist tongue cools the temperature of the blood flowing through the tongue. Similarly, the canary loses heat through its feathers. The temperature regulation centres in man are the **hypothalamus,** an area at the base of the brain, which functions like a thermostat.

A bird's body temperature is higher than that of a human being, and this high temperature is necessary to ensure that the bird is alert and ready for any eventuality. A bird's reactions are as quick and responsive as a well-tuned engine; only if the bird is warm and responsive can it react instantly should danger threaten.

With a bird, its plumage provides a very efficient insulation against loss of body temperature. The bird instinctively covers all the parts of the body with its feathers, and so maintains its constant body temperature. You will have seen birds standing on one leg with their beaks tucked into their feathers. By so doing, should the air temperature drop, the bird will still be able to breathe air which is almost at body temperature. It is for the same reason that a bird will stand on one leg, and the other one is tucked into its warm feathers.

CORNS

If a canary develops a corn on the ball of a foot, this can quickly be detected as the bird will hold up the affected foot while standing on a perch. First remove all the normal cage perches and replace them with a single round perch in the centre of which a large 'V' has been cut. This will avoid any pressure being put on the corn when it grips the perch. To cure or remove the corn, all that is required is to paint it thoroughly four or five times a day with iodine. This will result in the corn gradually becoming smaller and hard and you will be able to remove it with your fingernail. A bottle of **clear** iodine should always be kept handy in the birdroom as it is ideal to stop any form of bleeding from either broken skin or a broken flight or tail feathers.

INFECTIOUS DISEASES

In simple terms an infectious disease is one which can be transmitted through the environment from one animal to another. This is distinct from the non-infectious diseases that are seen in the individual without likelihood of spreading to others. Thus, influenza is infectious, rheumatism is not.

The risk of spread of infection obviously increases as population densities increase. This results from closer contact, more contamination, a higher 'reservoir' of initial infection and often environments favourable to transmission, i.e. humidity, common drinking and feeding utensils, and so on.

What are the Diseases of Importance?

There is not very much data available on the relative importance of the various diseases in cage birds, due to several factors including the relative ease of obtaining some treatments, e.g. de-worming agents, and the inability to get data from the total spectrum of husbandry types. In spite of this, the infectious diseases of most importance seem to be related to the intestinal tract and the respiratory tract (there are other groups of sickness of importance, e.g. physical injuries, reproductive failure, poor nutrition, and so on).

Bacterial diseases

There are a great number of bacteria types that may be truly pathogenic (disease producing) or are potentially pathogenic (cause diseases) if conditions become favourable. The ability of a particular bacteria species to produce disease varies from highly infectious to non-infectious. The development of disease depends on a breakdown of the bird's resistance to infection or subjecting the bird to an excessive challenge of infective agent. Once established, bacterial diseases can be rapidly fatal and fast spreading (particularly enteric and respiratory infections).

The only way to treat bacterial diseases is to select the correct drug and to administer sufficient of the drug to destroy the disease agent's superiority in the host bird and to administer the drug at the right site; e.g. if a disease state is restricted to the gastrointestinal tract then a gut retained treatment will suffice, such as with simple enteritis. If, however, the condition has progressed to the sick bird syndrome then further antibiotic therapy may be necessary (you invariably have access to good broad spectrum water soluble and readily absorbed antibiotics). It is critical, however, to use sufficient drug to resolve the infective state.

Viral diseases

There are several viral diseases affecting poultry and similar viral agents probably affect cage birds but have not as yet been reliably diagnosed. Viruses are simpler disease agents to bacteria and are pathogenic within cells. In general, if animals can survive the cellular destruction they can develop immunity to infection. Viral diseases tend to be highly infectious. Most of the damage results from subsequent bacterial infections and treatment is aimed at reducing this. In general we cannot treat viral diseases.

CANARY POX   —   The virus affects skin related tissues — beak, legs, feather follicles, etc.

             —   The virus particles are fairly resistant so spread is easy.

             —   Vaccines can be prepared but are hazardous to use.

             —   Treatment is aimed at hygiene and antibiotic support over period of risk.

Fungal diseases

There are several disease states that are associated with fungal agents — these fungi are opportunists and will not cause disease unless conditions favour their growth either in the bird or in their feed. The fungi may be directly disease producing, or their poisons in feed may cause damage in the bird (mycotoxins). Treatment can be successful using antimycotic drugs (best to use water soluble preparations) and good hygiene to reduce the challenge in the environment, i.e. dryness and good feed storage.

Parasitic diseases

There are many **ecto-** and **endo-parasites** that affect birds. All life forms that colonize a host are theoretically parasites but we tend to use the term to the helminth (worm) parasites, protozoa parasites, and the arthropod (insect and related group) parasites. They are 'disease producing' as evidenced by a depression in health status either as a direct effect or through diseases they can transmit. There are many disease states caused by these groups and again it is important to be aware of the causal agent, the drug of choice, the effective dose and any precautionary advice.

Preventive medicine

It is in the interest of both the bird and the owner to apply a few basic principles of preventive medicine to get an overall reduction in the incidence of general (simple) disease states. It is these general disease states that lower the bird's resistance and allow more serious and therefore more complicated conditions to arise. The following steps are important, yet very simple, ways of preventing disease.

1. Reduce stress

   Stress is the common factor in inducing and progressing a disease or potential disease. If you place a stressed bird in a theoretically adequate environment, it is more likely to succumb than a non-stressed bird. Stress factors include cold, heat, wetness (chilling), lack of air (oxygen), overcrowding, poor feeding, lack of water, fear of predator animals, boredom, poor hygiene, leading to the excess disease challenge.

2. Ensure adequate nutrition

   Briefly, the controls that you can exercise are:
   (a) good storage of feeds;
   (b) only use clean reliable seed (ask questions about its source and quality);
   (c) use a variety of feeds;
   (d) fresh feeds are better with respect to palatability, and vitamin levels.

3. Ensure adequate housing

   To reduce infectious diseases it is important to:
   (a) maintain a high level of cleanliness, i.e. thorough and regular periodic fumigation;
   (b) avoid overcrowding the birds;
   (c) reduce stresses by gradual introduction of the bird to the new environment;
   (d) apply quarantine procedures.

4. Reduce disease risks

   This can be done by:
   (a) regularly treating birds for certain disease states that may be present e.g. worms, coccidiosis, and so on;
   (b) using the medication at an effective level:
   (c) not using continuous therapy as this may promote resistance states in the population.

Figure 14.3 Giving a thorough spring cleaning

Conclusion

All of the infectious and contagious diseases have a common history of development in any aviary or birdroom situation. It is the role of the good manager to prevent the final result (the disease state) by stopping this common pathway at some stage. **The further back along the path this is effected, the better the result.**

179

CHAPTER 15

Guide-lines for Judges

JUDGES MUST HAVE CONFIDENCE

Certain conditions are most important when judging birds. There should, of course, be good, even lighting throughout the hall and all the cages should be at the correct height. Carrying the birds to and forth, particularly if they are brought from a dark spot at the back of the hall to a light spot, where they are being judged, can disturb them and they should be left for 10 minutes to settle and adjust to the lighting conditions under which they are to be judged.

Speedy judging is not desirable. On the other hand, too much time can be spent with individual birds, although sometimes the individual in question may be the best in show. However, it must be passed over for perfectly good reasons; the first impressions you get of a bird are generally a good guide to its potential.

The constant use of a judging stick is not always a good idea. I never use a judging stick, finding that the movement of the hand is quite sufficient to control the bird. Different judges, of course, adopt varying methods.

Procedure

I prefer to adopt a set procedure while judging. First, if there is a large class of birds to be judged, one should ensure that no bird is missing from the class, or wrongly classed. A good steward can be very helpful in this matter.

Secondly, if it is a young bird which is close-ringed, check for the current-year ring on the bird's leg. At the same time look for any missing toe nails or any other deformity of the feet.

Lastly, as I make my way along the class again, I usually look for the bird which at first appears to come up to the *standard*. I then place it in the position from which I wish to work.

It does not matter which way you work, it can be either from the right or left. Having selected the individual that you consider to be a good bird, compare it with the rest of its class and place them in position and re-check before making your decision and before marking up the cage label.

Figure 15.1 Crest Canary; very good crest and closely drawn on the legs

Take a further look to see how the canary conforms with the standard of perfection, which must always be kept in mind when judging:

(a) Type and shape of head, shape of body and wing carriage must be noted.

(b) Condition: good, tight feathering.

(c) The bird must not be too fat or too thin.

(d) The frontal view should show a good lift from the beak.

(e) The head should be round and full, with a good width between the eyes.

(f) The shoulders are to be full and wide and in proportion to the body.

181

(g) The back is to be in accordance with the body; the chest nicely rounded with a clean line right through from the beak to the tail.

(h) Good balance and position must be maintained at all times while perching; this is particularly important when judging Borders.

Dirty birds and cages should be penalised. When penalising a bird for these faults, I state the reason on the show cage label, so that the exhibitor knows why his bird has lost points and that it is his fault and not that of the bird.

Individuals showing good points should be moved from the left to the right or vice versa, depending on which way you are judging, and the birds with faults should be moved in the opposite direction. A further walk down the judging line is important before marking up your awards to ensure that a bird has not been passed the wrong way or been missed.

You will find some classes are very good in quality throughout, while others are quite poor and it can be most difficult to find a good bird among those on the judging table.

I find that the lesser quality birds are always by far the hardest to judge. Look for thin or missing feathers, or a bird with drooping wings, as wing carriage is very important in an exhibition canary, irrespective of its breed.

ESSENTIAL ATTRIBUTES

The following are necessary in an exhibition canary: a bold head (in proportion to the body), good feather condition throughout, a good, even colour and most importantly, a bird must be true to its type or variety. I would like to make the following comments:

(a) There is no such thing as a perfect bird.

(b) Never query your fellow judge in front of exhibitors.

(c) Judges can make mistakes, but just because a bird was placed first last week and did not get a ticket this week, it does not follow that it is the judge who is at fault.

(d) All that is asked of judges is for them to be honest in their opinions.

Never hesitate to change your decision if you find that you have missed something earlier, before finally marking up the awards. Concentrate the whole time during which you are judging. If you happen to lose your concentration, walk away for a little while and have a chat or take a break for five minutes or so. Calm down and when your mind is re-settled go back to the judging bench.

Figure 15.2 A show in progress

Ask for advice

Never hesitate to ask for advice, especially if you are adjudicating with another judge. If there is any doubt about a particular matter in the class that you are judging, it often pays to consult your fellow judge.

You must also have a good eye, not only for the bird you are judging, but also for colour, as this is of great importance especially when judging specials.

As I said before, you must have confidence in yourself the whole time you are judging. It is not always the man who remembers the points and every detail laid down in the standard of excellence who makes the best judge. Nor is it the exhibitor who exhibits the best bird in show who makes the best judge.

Excellent exhibitors

I know of several excellent exhibitors who, when judging, would not select as winners birds that they themselves would exhibit. In other words, we can all show something better than the other chap and he could show one even better. This is something which should be borne in mind at all times.

IN CONCLUSION

And now, finally, at the end of this book which has been based on forty-eight years' personal experience of breeding, exhibiting and judging of canaries in the United Kingdom, Spain, Australia and the U.S.A. To me this has been solely a 'hobby' which has made me many sincere friends in three continents of the world. I have not attempted to give you any set pairing to be used on a commercial basis as that is not the object of the book.

It is only natural that we all would like to be successful exhibitors, and to assist you to be so you should pay particular attention to what I have written in Chapter 4, for to me this is the key to being a successful breeder. I am quite sure that you will experience successes and disappointments, but this is what makes our hobby so very interesting; every unexpected experience — be it good or bad — is something new, and as the years go by they will give you much pleasure.

You will gradually learn not to expect immediate success, and you will become an optimist, which will help over times of disappointment and keep your feet on the ground when success comes along.

To introduce improvement in your stock will entail a detailed examination of what your objective is : I trust that this book will be of help to those who are new to the Fancy as well as the more experienced fanciers.

APPENDIX

CANARY TERMINOLOGY

ACTION:
Refers to a bird's movement in a show cage; particularly refers to Borders.

CARRIAGE:
Is the bearing, attitude and style of a bird in a show cage.

CHROMOSOMES:
Are microscopic gene-carrying bodies in the tissue of a cell, formed before cell divisions take place. The **XX** and **XY** chromosomes indicate a bird's sex, where the **XX** is a cock and **XY** a hen.

DRIVE:
Movement on the perch.

DOMINANT:
Is a quality which a bird possesses and passes on to its young.

FLIGHTS:
The primary quills, or the long outer feathers in the wing.

GENETICS:
Are a combination of two dominant factors, often referred to as the art of canary breeding.

GENES:
Are microscopic hereditary carrying factors for such features as colour, sex, feather quality and so on.

GRIZZLE:
Feathers that are streaked and intermingled which intensifies the finish of the feathers.

GROUND COLOUR:
The general colour of the body feathers.

LIGHT THROATED:
A fault in either a self green or cinnamon.

LIPOCHROME:
Are yellow or buff ground birds.

185

LONG IN THE BARREL: A term often used to describe a Norwich which is too long in the body.

MELANIN: Are green or cinnamon ground birds.

OVER SHOWN: A bird which has been exhibited at many shows, with the result that it is tired, has lost some of its drive and whose feather quality has lost its sparkle.

PENCILLING: The narrow lines of darker coloured feathers on the back and sides in self greens and cinnamons.

POSITION: The carriage of a bird when in a show cage.

QUALITY: An attribute to a bird's feather, condition, colour and type.

RECESSIVE: Can be described as negative recessive gene carried by a bird.

ROWINGS: These are the markings of a Lizard Canary on its breast.

SADDLE: That part of the back behind the shoulders.

SELF: A term applied to greens and cinnamons which have **no** light colour feathers at all.

SOFT: A feather indication that a bird is not its normal lively self.

SPANGLES: Are the markings in the feather on the back of a Lizard Canary.

STAMINA: Indicates a bird's health, strength and vigour.

STEADY: A term used to indicate a bird's behaviour and movement from perch to perch while in a show cage.

STRAIN: Normally refers to one particular fancier's birds who are all very similar to each other in type, and are all blood related.

186

SUBSTANCE:	Normally refers to the size of the body.
SWEATING:	A term used during the breeding season, when a hen has young in the nest, all of which have an appearance of their feathers being damp.
TAILING:	Is when the tail feathers of a nest feather bird are removed.
THICK SET:	Refers to the shape of the body; in the case of Norwich Canaries, birds which have a stout built appearance.
TICKED:	A bird which has a small dark mark, not exceeding the size of a modern one pence piece, on an otherwise completely clear bird, or if it has not got more than three dark feathers side by side in only one wing or tail.
TYPE:	Is the overall characteristic of a bird which resembles the **Standard of Excellence** for its breed.
UNFLIGHTED:	A current year bred bird which has not yet moulted its flight or tail feathers.
VARIEGATED:	Birds which have more light than dark feathers.
WORK:	A term generally used to describe good back spangling on a Lizard.

INDEX

Ailments, see Illnesses
Antibiotics, 91
Australia, 132, 162-7

B
Barcelona Canary Union Show, 131
Belgians, 34
Birdrooms, 138-41
Blue Borders, 127
Borders, 5-11, 106, 124
Border Fancy Canary Club, 5
Breeding, 40-8
  and egg structure 83-6
  faults 49-53
  and line breeding 71-2
  and out breeding 119
  and ovaries 79
  and test mating 77, 118-9

C
Cake, 160
Canary Isles, 1
Charcoal, 97, 154
Cinnamon Borders, 4, 124-6
Clear Borders, 3, 111-2
Condition, 92
Colour Production, 73-4
Crests, 31, 113
Cuttlefish, 159

Diet, 55-62
  and feeders, 157

E
Exhibiting
  and colour feeding, 105
  and hand-washing, 116
  and position, 113
  preparation, 115-8
  and show cages, 117-8, 129

F
Fawn Borders, 127
Feather Mite, 141

Feeding, see Diet
Fife Fancy, 34-6, 114
Fouls, 3

G
Genetics, 67-71
Glosters, 11-13, 109
  Australian Glosters, 163
  Corona Consort, 11
  Gloster Consort, 11
Green Borders, 3, 124
Greenfood, 57-8

H
Hartz Roller, 2
Havedoarn, DR. AL, 120
Hospital Cage, 117

I
Illness
  asthma, 171
  canary pox, 177
  colds, 171
  corns, 175
  enteritis, 170
  eye diseases, 171
  fungal diseases, 177
  'going light', 173
  hepatitis, 168
  loss of feathers, 173
  parasitic diseases, 177
  pneumonia, 169
  preventive medicine, 178
  respitory complaints, 169
  scaly legs and feet, 173
  stiff hind claw, 172
  thrush, 171
  toenails, 173
  viral diseases, 177

L
Lancashire Coppy, 36-7, 114
Laying difficulties, 47
Lime water, 158

Lipochrome colouring, 23
Lizard Canaries, 20-3, 110
Lizard Canary Association, 21
London Fancy, 38-9

M
Melanins, 29
Melanistic colouring, 23

N
Nesting
   and nestboxes, 64
   preparation, 137
New colours, 23, 111
Norwich canaries, 13-16, 109-10
Norwich Plainhead Club (N P C), 13

P
Pairing, 65

R
Red Borders, 28
Red Mite, 47
Roller Canaries, 3, 20
Rose-hip syrup, 166

S
Scotch Fancy, 31-33, 113
Seed, 57
   blue maw, 147
   canary seed, 146
   lettuce seed, 148
   linseed, 143-4
   gold of pleasure seed, 148
   hemp seed, 150
   niger seed, 149
   persicaria seed, 152
   rope seed, 57, 100, 147
   shepherd's purse seed, 150
   sprouted seed, 62, 159
   teazle seed, 148
Selfs, 3, 111
Sexing, 45
Shell-grit, 156
Show features, 54
Smith, A W, 11

Softfood, 61, 153
South Africa, 132
Standards of Excellence, 5
Stock selection, 65

T
Ticked birds, 3
Type canaries, 128-34

W
White Borders, 124, 126-7
Wild canaries, 1

V
Variegated birds, 3

Y
Yorkshire canaries, 17-19, 110